Negotiation Beyond the Playbook™

Principles, Pitfalls, and Pointers

C. Richard Barnes

 Printed in the U.S.A.

FIRST EDITION

DEDICATION

To my wife of 45 years, Audrey - known to many as "The Lovely Mrs. Barnes."

Long before there was a book, before the stories, the lessons, and the long hours spent helping others find their way through difficult conversations... there was you.

You have been my steady ground in an unsteady profession. The quiet voice of reason when I had heard enough noise for one day.

The reminder that patience, grace, and perspective are not just tools of negotiation - they are the foundation of a life well lived.

You have supported this journey in ways most will never see - through late nights, long absences from home, and more stories than any one person should have to listen to twice.

This book carries my name, but it is built on a lifetime we have shared. for your unwavering support, your strength, your humor, and your love I dedicate this book to you.

Love, Richard

Table of Contents

INTRODUCTION

After decades spent in conference rooms, job trailers, union halls, boardrooms, mediation tables, and tense conference calls where voices were raised and stakes were high, one thing becomes clear: negotiation is rarely what people think it is.

Most people imagine negotiation as a contest of persuasion. Someone makes a demand, the other side pushes back, and the exchange becomes a tug-of-war over numbers, terms, or authority. Books often present negotiation as a series of tactics, anchors, concessions, leverage points, and closing moves. These tools have their place. But over time, negotiators learn that the real work happens somewhere deeper than tactics.

Negotiation is not merely the exchange of proposals. It is the management of pressure, perception, and human identity under conditions of uncertainty.

Every negotiation contains layers. On the surface are positions. Beneath those positions are interests. And beneath those interests lie the powerful emotional forces that shape human behavior, fear of loss, desire for respect, pressure from constituents, and the quiet calculation of what the future might hold.

Over the years I have watched negotiations fail, not because agreement was impossible, but because the participants misunderstood the nature of the conflict they were trying to resolve. They tried to win arguments instead of managing the dynamics of that conflict.

The material in these pages is organized around three ideas that experienced negotiators learn through practice: Principles, Pitfalls, and Pointers.

- Principles are the enduring realities of negotiation. They explain how conflict behaves, how pressure develops, and how people respond when identity, reputation, or loss is at stake.
- Pitfalls are the mistakes negotiators repeatedly make, even experienced ones. These errors often arise not from lack of intelligence, but from human instincts that work against us in moments of tension.
- Pointers are practical ways to navigate these realities. They are not tricks or manipulations. Rather, they are disciplined habits of thinking and communication that allow negotiators to remain steady while others become reactive.

The insights that follow examine the strategic dynamics that shape real negotiations: loss aversion, reactive devaluation, ego investment, constituent pressure, identity-based conflict, emotions, and the challenge of knowing when to escalate - or when to step back.

These perspectives often run counter to the way negotiation is taught in quick seminars or summarized in business books promising simple formulas. Real negotiation is messier than that. It involves personalities, power dynamics, time pressures, and the ever-present possibility that someone's pride or fear will derail the conversation. Yet, within that complexity, patterns exist. Those patterns are what this book explores.

The goal here is not to produce perfect negotiators. No such people exist. Even experienced professionals make mistakes when pressure rises or assumptions go unchallenged. The goal is something more practical: to help you recognize what is happening in the room while it is happening.

When you can see those dynamics clearly, when you understand why a conversation is hardening, or why an offer is being rejected, you gain the ability to respond deliberately instead of reactively. That is the difference between negotiation as a contest and negotiation as a craft.

This book is not meant to be read once and shelved, it is built as a working reference library for real-world negotiation. Each Chapter and each Insight stand on their own as a practical entry point.

C. Richard Barnes

CHAPTER ONE

THE REALITY BENEATH THE RITUAL

"Negotiation rarely derails because of numbers. It derails because of emotion."

Insight #1. Negotiation Is Not Just a Meeting

Insight #2. You Are Always Negotiating

Insight #3. The Myth of Win-Win

Insight #4. Power, Rights and Interest - The Three Lenses

Insight #5. The Emotional Undercurrent

Insight #6. Face, Ego and Status on the Job-Site

Insight #7. Availability Bias in Real-Time Decisions

Insight #8. The Danger of the Single-Issue Frame

Insight #9. Decomposing the Mess Before You Solve It

Insight #10. Negotiating In Layers, Not All at Once

INSIGHT 1 – NEGOTIATION IS NOT JUST A MEETING

In many organizations, negotiation is treated as an event on the calendar. A meeting is scheduled, participants gather around a table, positions are presented, and everyone expects that by the end of the hour something will be resolved. This view is convenient, but it is fundamentally wrong.

Seasoned negotiators understand something that inexperienced ones often miss: negotiation is not the meeting. The meeting is merely one moment inside a much longer process. Real negotiation begins long before people sit down together and continues long after they leave the room.

The danger of confusing the two is subtle but significant. When people think negotiation happens only during the meeting, they focus on what to say instead of what to understand, who is involved, and how decisions are actually made. They prepare arguments instead of preparing strategy.

The most effective negotiators recognize that the meeting is simply the visible portion of a deeper process involving preparation, relationship management, timing, and influence across multiple conversations.

The Principle

Negotiation is a process, not an event.

Experienced negotiators know that by the time people sit down at the table, much of the negotiation has already happened. Interests have been formed. Stakeholders have discussed the issue privately. Expectations have been set. Informal conversations have shaped what people believe is possible. In many cases, the outcome has already begun to take shape before the formal discussion ever begins.

The meeting itself is simply where the visible exchange occurs.

A seasoned negotiator spends far more time working outside the meeting than inside it. They gather information. They understand the pressures affecting each party. They identify who truly influences the decision and who merely occupies a seat at the table.

They also recognize that people rarely change their views in public settings. In meetings, individuals tend to defend positions because they are being observed by colleagues, superiors, or constituents. Public environments encourage rigidity.

Real movement often happens elsewhere—in hallway conversations, follow-up calls, or quiet discussions where people feel less exposed.

This does not mean the meeting is unimportant. Meetings serve several purposes. They signal seriousness, allow parties to hear one another directly, and provide structure to the process. But they are not where negotiation begins, nor where it typically ends.

The skilled negotiator treats the meeting as one instrument within a broader strategy, not the strategy itself.

The Pitfall

Over-preparing for the conversation and under-preparing for the context.

One of the most common mistakes negotiators make is spending all their energy preparing what they will say in the meeting. They craft arguments. They organize talking points. They anticipate objections and they rehearse responses.

But they neglect the deeper preparation that actually determines success.

They do not fully understand who the decision-makers are. They underestimate the influence of people who are not present and they fail to explore concerns before positions become hardened in public.

As a result, the meeting becomes an arena for debate rather than a platform for progress.

This mistake is especially common in professional environments where meetings dominate the culture. Organizations are accustomed to solving problems through formal discussions, so people assume negotiation will follow the same pattern.

But negotiation rarely works that way.

If the first time someone hears about an issue is in the meeting itself, resistance is almost guaranteed. People instinctively defend themselves when they feel surprised, pressured, or unprepared.

Likewise, if stakeholders arrive without having explored possible solutions privately, the conversation quickly becomes positional. Participants stake out territory rather than search for workable outcomes.

The meeting becomes a performance instead of a negotiation.

When this happens, negotiators often conclude that the other side is being unreasonable. In reality, the problem is usually structural: too much weight was placed on the meeting itself and too little attention was given to the process surrounding it.

The Pointer

Work the ground before you work the table.

Seasoned negotiators understand that the most productive meetings are rarely spontaneous. They are the result of deliberate groundwork.

Before the meeting occurs, they invest time in understanding the environment surrounding the negotiation. They ask questions quietly and early, they test ideas in smaller conversations, and they identify concerns before they become public objections.

These preliminary discussions are not manipulative. They are clarifying. They allow people to explore possibilities without committing themselves in front of an audience.

By the time the formal meeting occurs, fewer surprises remain.

Skilled negotiators also think carefully about who should be present and who should not. Sometimes progress requires bringing additional voices into the conversation. Other times it requires limiting the number of participants so people can speak candidly.

Timing matters as well. Calling a meeting too early - before interests and constraints are understood - often guarantees frustration. Waiting until groundwork has been laid creates conditions where the meeting can actually accomplish something.

Finally, seasoned negotiators recognize that the process continues after the meeting ends. Agreements must be communicated, interpreted, and sometimes renegotiated as circumstances evolve. They follow up, they reinforce understanding, and they address lingering concerns before they grow into new conflicts.

In other words, they manage the negotiation as a process rather than a single encounter. When negotiators adopt this mindset, meetings begin to function differently. Instead of being arenas where sides clash, they become checkpoints in a longer conversation. The pressure decreases. The discussion becomes more constructive. And outcomes become far more durable.

In reality, the most important work in negotiation rarely happens at the table. It happens before the meeting begins—and after everyone leaves the room.

INSIGHT 2 – YOU ARE ALWAYS NEGOTIATING

Most people think negotiation begins when two parties sit down at a table to discuss terms. In reality, negotiation begins long before anyone says the word deal. It begins in everyday interactions when expectations are set, when authority is exercised or when

trust is quietly built or eroded. Negotiation is not an event; it is an environment. It begins the moment two people's interests intersect.

On a construction site, in a boardroom, at a kitchen table, in a union hall, you are always negotiating. Not always about money. Not always about contracts. But always about something: time, attention, priorities, authority, risk, respect, or identity. You may not call it negotiation. But it is.

The Principle

Every interaction is an exchange of interests.

Negotiation is not an event; it is a condition of human interaction. Whenever someone wants something, someone controls something, or two people see the same situation differently you are negotiating.

When a foreman asks for another crew for Friday, he's negotiating resources. When a project manager pushes back on a change order, she's negotiating risk allocation. When a superintendent decides whether to escalate or resolve quietly, he's negotiating reputation and relationships.

Silence negotiates, tone negotiates, even timing negotiates. You are constantly signaling what you value, what you will tolerate, what you will resist and what you are willing to trade.

The seasoned negotiator understands something fundamental: leverage is built long before the formal meeting.

- Your credibility.
- Your consistency.
- Your emotional control.
- Your reputation for fairness.
- Your history of follow-through.

All of it negotiates on your behalf before you ever open your mouth. If negotiation is only something you "turn on" during disputes, you are already late.

The Pitfall

Thinking negotiation only happens at the table.

The most common mistake is believing negotiation starts when the meeting starts. By the time the formal conversation begins, much has already been decided:

- Expectations have formed.
- Coalitions have aligned.
- Narratives have spread.
- Emotional positions have hardened.

If you ignore the everyday negotiations - the hallway conversations, the email tone, the way you handle small disputes - you surrender influence in the moments that matter most.

Consider this job-site moment: A subcontractor raises minor concerns week after week. The superintendent dismisses them casually. Nothing dramatic. No formal dispute. Just subtle signals: “We’ll see.” “That’s not our issue.” “Handle it.”

Months later, a major change order explodes. Now both sides are dug in. But the negotiation didn’t begin with the change order. It began with those small, unaddressed conversations. Every ignored issue negotiates distrust. Every sarcastic comment negotiates resentment, and every delayed callback negotiates disrespect.

By the time the “real” negotiation arrives, the emotional ledger is already full.

The Pointer

Negotiate intentionally - even when it feels informal.

If you are always negotiating, then you must always be deliberate. This does not mean you treat every conversation like a courtroom battle. It means you stay aware of the exchange happening beneath the surface.

Three practical shifts make the difference:

1. Guard Your Signals.
    - Your reactions teach people how to approach you.
    - If you flare up, people negotiate around you.
    - If you ignore problems, people escalate past you.

- If you listen calmly and respond predictably, people negotiate with you.
- You are training others every day.

2. Think Long-Term Equity, Not Short-Term Wins.
    - Winning a minor argument at the cost of credibility is a losing trade.
    - Publicly embarrassing a partner may win the moment but lose the relationship.
    - Ask yourself: What reputation am I negotiating right now?
3. Slow Down Before You Respond.
    - Most negotiation damage happens in reflex.
    - An impulsive email.
    - A sharp retort.
    - A dismissive gesture.
    - Pausing is power.

When you slow your response, you widen your options. And when you widen your options, you increase your leverage. Intentional negotiators are rarely the loudest. They are rarely the most aggressive. They are rarely the fastest to react, but they are the most aware.

The powerful negotiator does not "turn it on" when the stakes rise. They live in a way that builds leverage daily. They manage tone, relationships, expectations, and credibility continuously.

The real negotiation is not the dramatic meeting. It is the steady accumulation of trust, influence, and reputation long before that meeting ever occurs. You are always negotiating. The only question is whether you are doing it consciously – or letting it happen to you.

INSIGHT 3 – THE MYTH OF WIN–WIN

Negotiation folklore loves a clean ending: both sides smile, shake hands, and walk away declaring victory. The banner over the table reads win-win, and everyone feels virtuous. But seasoned negotiators know something uncomfortable - every negotiation

involves trade-offs, and trade-offs mean someone gives something up.

The myth of win-win isn't that mutual benefit is impossible. It's that agreement must feel equally good to both sides at the same time. That expectation distorts judgment, delays decisions, and sometimes kills perfectly workable deals.

The Principle

Value is created in differences, not symmetry.

True negotiation leverage comes from differences in priorities, risk tolerance, time horizons, and constraints.

If two parties value everything equally, there's nothing to trade. A contractor may value schedule flexibility more than short-term margin. An owner may value cost certainty more than speed. A union may value predictability over incremental wage gains. These differences are not obstacles. They are the raw material of agreement.

A sophisticated negotiator doesn't chase emotional parity - "Do you feel like you won?" - but structural alignment - "Did we trade intelligently?" Win-win, properly understood, doesn't mean equal gain. It means optimal exchange.

Sometimes one side wins more on price while the other wins more on timing. Sometimes one side wins visibly while the other wins quietly in risk allocation. The scoreboard only looks equal if you understand what was truly at stake. The goal is not for both parties to feel euphoric. The goal is for both parties to prefer the deal over their alternatives.

That is the real measure of success.

The Pitfall

Forcing fairness theater.

The biggest mistake negotiators make is performing "fairness theater."

They chase cosmetic balance instead of substantive value. They split differences reflexively. They soften positions just to preserve optics. They apologize for winning a concession they legitimately earned and in doing so, they distort incentives.

Splitting the difference feels civilized - but it often

ignores underlying interests. It can reward extreme opening positions and punish reasonable ones. It can create artificial compromise where none was required.

Worse, the obsession with everyone feeling like a winner can block necessary tension.

Sometimes one side genuinely has more leverage. Sometimes market conditions favor one party and sometimes one side made a strategic error earlier in the process.

Pretending those realities don't exist doesn't create fairness. It creates fragility. Deals built on emotional symmetry rather than economic clarity tend to unravel later. They manifest in performance disputes, change orders, or in future rounds of negotiation. The unresolved imbalance doesn't disappear; it resurfaces.

Another hidden cost of win-win mythology is decision paralysis. If negotiators believe both sides must feel equally enthusiastic, they hold out for perfection. They wait for a moment where no discomfort exists.

That moment rarely comes.

All durable agreements contain some degree of tension. If neither side feels any pressure, it's possible value was left on the table.

The Pointer

Define success by alternatives, not emotions.

Seasoned negotiators anchor their definition of success to one question: compared to what? Compared to litigation, delay, re-bidding the project, striking, or walking away?

A deal is successful if it beats the alternative - not if it generates applause.

This requires clarity about leverage and BATNA (Best Alternative to a Negotiated Agreement), but it also requires emotional discipline. You must tolerate the fact that the other side may not look thrilled. They may feel stretched or pressured. They may feel like they conceded too much.

But that doesn't automatically mean the deal is unfair. The pointer here is to separate satisfaction from sustainability.

Ask:

- Does this agreement allocate risk intentionally?
- Are the trade-offs explicit?
- Do both parties understand what they gained and what they gave?
- Is this better than the realistic alternative?

If the answer is yes, you likely have a strong agreement - even if no one is celebrating.

Another practical pointer: articulate the trades clearly before closing. Instead of saying, "So we're agreed," say: "We're taking on the schedule risk, and in exchange you're giving us price protection."

Or: "You're getting longer contract duration, and we're getting predictability."

When trades are named, value becomes visible. When value is visible, the need for symbolic equality fades.

The most durable agreements are rarely cinematic. They are pragmatic. Both sides leave knowing they didn't get everything. Both sides understand why the other pushed. Both sides calculate that moving forward is wiser than escalating.

That is not naïve win-win. It is disciplined exchange. Negotiation is not about manufacturing mutual exhilaration. It is about engineering mutually preferable outcomes under constraint.

The myth of win-win seduces people into thinking conflict

can disappear. It cannot, but it can be structured. Trade-offs can be optimized and value can be exchanged intelligently.

That is not failure, that is negotiation.

INSIGHT 4 – POWER, RIGHTS, AND INTERESTS — THE THREE LENSES

Negotiation is rarely a single conversation about a single issue. It is a layered interaction shaped by leverage, legitimacy, and need. Seasoned negotiators learn to look at every conflict through three distinct lenses: power, rights, and interests. Each lens clarifies something essential. Each, when misused, distorts judgment. Mastery lies not in choosing one lens but in knowing when to shift among them.

The Principle

Diagnose before you decide.

Every negotiation contains elements of power, rights, and interests.

Power is the ability to impose cost or withhold benefit. It is leverage. It is alternatives. It is time pressure, authority, market scarcity, reputation, relationships, and political capital. Power answers the question: What can I do if we don't agree?

Rights are standards of legitimacy. They include contracts, policies, laws, precedents, industry norms, and moral claims. Rights answer the question: What is fair or enforceable?

Interests are the underlying needs, fears, priorities, and motivations that drive positions. Interests answer the question: Why does this matter?

Most negotiators collapse these into one. They argue interests as if they were rights. They invoke rights when they lack power. They brandish power when they cannot win on fairness.

The seasoned negotiator separates them. When someone says, "We deserve a change order," that may be a rights claim. When they say, "We can't proceed without payment," that may be a power move. When they say, "We're worried about absorbing this risk," that is likely an interest.

The principle is simple: Diagnose the lens being used before you respond.

Responding to power with moral outrage escalates. Responding to interests with legal arguments frustrates. Responding to rights with threats destabilizes.

Each lens has its place. Interests build durable agreements. Rights resolve disputes when trust falters.

Power ends deadlock when nothing else works. The order matters. Start with interests. Move to rights if needed. Use power carefully – and last.

The Pitfall

Fighting in the wrong frame.

Negotiations deteriorate when parties fight in mismatched lenses. One side talks interest: "We need schedule flexibility because of supply chain delays." The other counters with rights: "The contract says liquidated damages apply."

Now both feel unheard. The first believes their reality is being ignored. The second believes the rules are being dismissed.

Escalation often follows a predictable path. When interests fail, parties argue rights. When rights fail, they reach for power. Each step increases cost and reduces relationship. The most common mistake is assuming that invoking rights or power makes you strong. Often it signals weakness.

When you lean too quickly on rights, you communicate that you cannot persuade on merit. When you threaten power too early, you reveal anxiety about losing control. The other side responds defensively. Positions harden and trust thins.

Some negotiators live in the power frame. Every issue is leverage. Every silence is strategy. Every concession is weakness. They may win short-term concessions, but they create long-term resistance.

Others cling to rights. They quote clauses and precedents as if authority alone creates agreement. But rights determine who is correct, not what is workable.

Still others stay exclusively in interests. They explore

feelings and need but avoid hard boundaries. They risk being perceived as naive or easily pressured.

The pitfall is not using any of these lenses. The pitfall is using only one. When negotiators fail to shift frames appropriately, they escalate prematurely or concede unnecessarily. They mistake moral certainty for strategy. They confuse volume with leverage. They argue fairness when the other side is calculating alternatives. Misdiagnosis leads to miscalculation.

The Pointer

Sequence with discipline.

The seasoned negotiator sequences the lenses deliberately.

First, surface the interests. Ask, "Help me understand what's driving this."

Listen for risk, pressure, identity, deadlines, internal politics. Most durable agreements are built here. Interests create options.

Second, clarify rights carefully. If alignment stalls, bring in standards: "How have we handled this before?" "What does the contract say?" Rights create boundaries and guardrails. They provide legitimacy without immediate escalation.

Third, assess power quietly. Before you threaten, evaluate. What are your real alternatives? What are theirs? How credible is any action? Power is strongest when it is visible but unused. Once deployed, it cannot be easily withdrawn.

This sequencing preserves relationship while protecting position. There are moments when power must be exercised. There are moments when rights must be asserted firmly. But disciplined negotiators treat power as a stabilizer, not a weapon; rights as a framework, not a shield; and interests as the primary engine of agreement.

They also watch for shifts. When the other party escalates to rights, it often signals fear. When they escalate to power, it often signals perceived loss. Instead of reacting symmetrically, the skilled negotiator may drop back down a lens: "It sounds like this feels risky to you. Let's talk about that."

Shifting downward in intensity often regains control.

Ultimately, the three lenses are not tactics. They are diagnostic tools. Power determines what is possible without agreement. Rights determine what is defensible. Interests determine what is sustainable.

Negotiation maturity is not about dominating one lens. It is about knowing which lens the moment requires - and having the discipline to use the least escalatory one that still protects your position.

When you see clearly through power, rights, and interests, you stop reacting emotionally to surface arguments. You start responding strategically to underlying dynamics and that is where negotiation stops being a contest of positions and becomes a deliberate act of leadership.

INSIGHT 5 – THE EMOTIONAL UNDERCURRENT

Negotiation is rarely derailed by numbers. It is derailed by emotion.

The conversation may appear to revolve around facts, timelines or specific demands, but people are often reacting to something deeper - respect, fear, pride, blame, identity, and status. These emotions rarely announce themselves directly. Instead, they surface through tone, posture, impatience, defensiveness or sudden rigidity in position.

When that undercurrent goes unmanaged, logic cannot save you. When it is understood and navigated well, you create what feels like a "win" long before ink hits paper. Recognizing this emotional undercurrent does not mean turning the negotiation into a therapy session. It means understanding that emotion is information. It signals where pressure exists, where trust may be fragile, and where a person feels their interests or their identity are being threatened. Skilled negotiators listen for these signals and adjust accordingly, addressing concern with calm acknowledgement rather than escalating tension.

The negotiator who can read and manage the emotional undercurrent gains a significant advantage. They remain steady when others become reactive.

The Principle

Emotion is not noise in negotiation. It is data.

The seasoned negotiator understands that raised voices, rigid positions, and abrupt ultimatums are not the real problem. They are signals.

Emotion tells you where someone feels threatened, where identity is at stake, where loss feels imminent, and where respect feels compromised.

In construction environments—where schedules are tight, margins thin, and reputations are hard-earned, emotion moves fast. A superintendent who says, "We're not paying for that change order," may actually mean, "If I approve this, I'll look incompetent to my leadership." A subcontractor who snaps, "You guys never own your mistakes," may really be saying, "We're bleeding cash and nobody sees it."

The emotional undercurrent often determines whether a negotiation becomes collaborative or combative. Winning, in this sense, is not about dominating the other side. It is about stabilizing the emotional climate so that rational problem-solving can occur. A calm room produces better agreements.

The Pitfall

Arguing the facts while ignoring the feelings.

The common mistake is to double down on logic when emotion spikes.

Consider this construction-specific scenario:

A general contractor and a mechanical subcontractor are negotiating a substantial change order on a hospital project. The sub claims $420,000 for redesign and overtime caused by late owner decisions. The GC believes only $250,000 is justified.

In the meeting, the subcontractor's project manager says, "We've carried this job for six months because your team can't make decisions." The GC immediately responds with documentation: emails, meeting minutes, RFI logs. "That's not accurate. We responded within contractual timeframes." Now both sides are arguing about who is right.

But the real issue is not the paperwork. The subcontractor feels financially exposed and disrespected. They believe they absorbed risk that wasn't theirs. Their pride and survival instinct are activated. The GC feels accused and professionally attacked. Their competence and leadership identity are threatened.

As both sides defend themselves, the conversation hardens. Each new fact feels like another blow. The more one side explains, the more the other feels dismissed. Emotion escalates, positions calcify, and trust erodes.

The pitfall is thinking that better evidence solves emotional friction. It does not. Facts resolve issues. Emotion determines whether issues can be resolved.

The Pointer

Name the emotion without validating the accusation.

The seasoned negotiator does something counterintuitive: they slow down and surface what is beneath the surface. In the hospital project example, instead of countering the accusation, the GC might say: "It sounds like you feel you've been carrying costs that shouldn't have been yours - and that's creating real pressure for your team."

Notice what this does: it does not concede liability, it does not agree with the claim, yet it acknowledges the emotional reality.

Often, that single move lowers the temperature. When people feel heard, they stop fighting to be understood.

From there, the GC might continue: "Before we debate numbers, let's make sure we understand where the financial strain is coming from." Now the conversation shifts from accusation to exploration. The emotional undercurrent has been stabilized enough for analysis to begin.

Another pointer is to separate identity from the issue. Instead of debating "who failed," shift to "what conditions produced this outcome." In construction, that might mean reviewing decision timelines jointly rather than defensively.

The experienced negotiator also watches their own emotional triggers. Construction culture rewards toughness. But reacting sharply to a sharp comment only deepens the spiral.

Calm is contagious. When one party refuses to escalate, the emotional momentum changes direction. If a subcontractor walks away feeling respected - even if the number is not everything they wanted - the relationship remains intact. If they feel dismissed - even if they get the full dollar amount - the partnership erodes.

In long-term construction relationships, reputation and repeat work often outweigh a single negotiation result.

Remember, a win is not just a favorable number. It's preserving credibility, protecting working relationships, stabilizing the team and avoiding escalation into claims or litigation.

On complex projects, you will negotiate again, next week, next month, or next phase. If the emotional undercurrent is polluted, every future negotiation becomes harder. If it is managed well, you build a reputation as someone who can handle pressure without becoming pressure.

Where stakes are high and margins narrow, mastering the emotional undercurrent is not soft skill fluff. It is strategic leverage. The seasoned negotiator does not ignore emotion.

They read it, regulate it, and use it.

INSIGHT 6 – FACE, EGO AND STATUS ON THE JOB-SITE

On a construction site, concrete and steel are not the only things under load. So are identity, pride, and professional standing.

Foremen guard credibility. Superintendents guard authority. Trades guard reputation and jurisdiction. And when any of those feel threatened, negotiations derail - not because of money or schedule, but because of "face." Construction environments operate on visible competence and reputation. When someone is corrected publicly, challenged aggressively, or made to appear incompetent in front of the crew, the dispute quickly stops being about the task and becomes about protecting identity. What could have been a simple clarification turns into a standoff, because "face" is threatened and people defend their standing as fiercely as they defend their position.

If you miss this dynamic, you misdiagnose the conflict.

The Principle

Protect "face" to protect the deal.

"Face" is public identity. It is how a person believes they are seen - competent, respected, in control. On a jobsite, "face" is currency. Lose it publicly, and cooperation collapses.

Ego is not vanity. It is self-protection. Status is not arrogance. It is positioning within a hierarchy that determines who gets heard and who gets sidelined.

On a construction project, status is everywhere:

- The general contractor running the meeting.
- The trade foreman defending crew productivity.
- The project manager guarding margin.
- The inspector asserting authority.

When someone feels diminished in front of their crew or peers, the brain shifts from problem-solving to self-defense. That is when positions harden.

The seasoned negotiator understands: threaten the person, and the problem gets worse. Protect the person, and the problem gets solvable. Saving "face" is not weakness. It is strategy.

This does not mean surrendering standards. It means correcting privately instead of publicly. It means framing adjustments as joint problem-solving instead of unilateral correction. It means giving people a dignified path to change course.

On a job-site, respect is oxygen. Remove it, and everything suffocates.

The Pitfall

Public correction and status games.

The common mistake is public confrontation.

Picture this: A framing crew is behind schedule. During the weekly coordination meeting, the superintendent says, "Your crew is killing this schedule. You're the reason we're slipping."

The room goes silent. The foreman feels exposed. His authority in front of his crew and peers is threatened. His response is predictable: "We're not the problem. We didn't get drawings on time. And your site logistics are a mess." Now, it is no longer about framing productivity. It is about status. Voices rise. Blame circulates. Each side digs in - not to solve the delay, but to avoid losing standing.

Another version is more subtle: sarcasm in front of others. Eye-rolling, dismissing someone's concern mid-sentence or rewriting commitments without conversation. These are status plays. They communicate, "You're not in control here."

The pitfall is assuming the other side is being difficult because of stubbornness or incompetence. In reality, they may simply be defending their professional identity. When people feel small, they act large. When they feel disrespected, they resist. And once the negotiation becomes about ego, cost and schedule become secondary.

The Pointer

Give status before you ask for concession.

The seasoned negotiator flips the instinct. Instead of asserting dominance, they establish respect first.

Back to the framing example. The superintendent could say, privately: "I know your crew has been pushing hard. I also know this slab delay hit everyone. Help me understand what's slowing your production so we can protect both of us."

Notice what happened: Competence was acknowledged, responsibility was shared, and the conversation moved from accusation to joint problem-solving. Status was preserved.

Another powerful move is to let the other side present the solution. Instead of declaring, "You need to add manpower," ask, "What would it take to recover three days without burning your crew out?" When someone authors the fix, they retain dignity.

Publicly, seasoned negotiators are careful with tone. They redirect rather than rebuke:

"Let's step back and focus on what gets us back on track." "Sounds like there are multiple factors here. Let's separate them."

They do not win points in the room. They build credibility over time.

There is also strategic use of private conversations. If correction is necessary, do it offstage. Protect the individual in front of others, and address the issue one-on-one. People rarely resist change when their identity is intact.

And sometimes, saving face means giving symbolic wins - allowing the other party to frame the final agreement, acknowledging their contribution in the meeting recap, or publicly recognizing their team's effort. Small gestures stabilize status. Stabilized status enables cooperation.

The most respected leaders on a jobsite are rarely the loudest or most dominant. They are the ones who create psychological safety while maintaining clear standards. They separate firmness from humiliation. They understand that preserving "face" is not about politeness - it is about momentum.

The goal is not to eliminate ego. That is impossible. Pride fuels craftsmanship. Status motivates performance. Reputation drives accountability. The goal is to manage it.

INSIGHT 7 – AVAILABILITY BIAS IN REAL-TIME DECISIONS

In construction, decisions are rarely made in quiet rooms with whiteboards and coffee. They are made in mud, noise, heat, and compressed time. Under those conditions, the human mind reaches

for what is most available, not what is most accurate. That instinct has a name: availability bias.

Availability bias is the tendency to judge likelihood and risk based on what comes most easily to mind. The most recent accident. The loudest complaint. The last project that went sideways. In real-time decisions, what is vivid often feels true. What are memorable feels probable, and what feels probable drives action.

The problem is not that experience influences judgment. The problem is when recent memory overrides balanced analysis.

The Principle

What is vivid is not always valid.

In fast-moving environments, the brain substitutes recall for research. If a similar event happened recently, it feels likely to happen again. If you have not seen something in a while, it feels rare even if the data says otherwise.

On a job-site, this plays out in predictable ways.

Imagine a superintendent who just finished a project where a concrete pour failed because of improper curing during an unexpected cold snap. The memory is fresh, costly, and embarrassing. Two months later, on a different project, temperatures are forecast to dip slightly overnight. It's nowhere near the prior severity, but the memory of the last failure is vivid.

The pour is halted. Subcontractors are frustrated. The schedule slips. Overtime costs rise. Objectively, the conditions do not justify the shutdown. But subjectively, the last failure is screaming in his head. The brain says: "Remember what happened last time."

The principle is simple: the ease of recall is not a reliable measure of probability. Seasoned leaders understand that recent experience feels heavier than older data. They do not ignore instinct - but they test it.

The Pitfall

Managing by the last crisis.

Availability bias turns leadership reactive.

After a fall incident, every toolbox talk becomes about ladders even if electrical hazards are statistically higher. After one aggressive subcontractor dispute, every firm negotiation is interpreted as a threat. After one project that went over budget because of steel escalation, every future steel quote is treated with suspicion.

The mind overcorrects. In negotiations, this is particularly dangerous. If the last union meeting ended in confrontation, the next one is approached defensively. Tone tightens. Assumptions harden. Neutral statements are heard as hostile. The past hijacks the present.

The pitfall is not learning from experience. The pitfall is overweighting the most recent, most emotional example and treating it as the norm.

Construction amplifies this bias because consequences are tangible and public. A crane malfunction, a failed inspection, a lost bid - these events carry financial and reputational sting. The stronger the emotion, the stronger the imprint. And the stronger the imprint, the more "available" it becomes in future decisions.

Left unchecked, availability bias narrows perspective. Leaders begin solving for yesterday's problem instead of today's reality.

The Pointer

Slow the frame, not the work.

You cannot eliminate availability bias. You can only counterbalance it. Seasoned construction leaders build small pauses into big decisions. Not long delays - just disciplined checks.

When a recent memory is driving urgency, they ask three questions:

1. Is this event statistically common, or just recently painful?
2. What does the data across multiple projects say?
3. If the last incident had not occurred, would I decide differently?

That third question is powerful. It separates pattern from panic.

Returning to the concrete example: a seasoned superintendent would still respect the prior failure, but would pull temperature forecasts, consult curing specifications, and review mitigation options before halting the pour. He might add thermal blankets instead of shutting down entirely. He responds proportionally, not emotionally.

In negotiation, the same discipline applies. If the last meeting was hostile, the seasoned negotiator does not assume hostility is inevitable. He prepares thoroughly, sets clear agendas, and resets tone deliberately. He refuses to let the most recent memory define the next interaction.

Another practical pointer is to track trends visually. Many firms maintain dashboards for safety, cost variance, and schedule performance. Data over time weakens the grip of lived experiences. When leaders see twelve months of numbers instead of one dramatic event, perspective returns.

Finally, diversify input. Availability bias thrives in isolation. When one person's recent experience dominates the room, decisions skew. Invite project managers, safety officers, estimators and ask: "What are you seeing across your projects?" Broader exposure dilutes narrow recall.

Real-time decisions will always rely partly on instinct. In construction, waiting for perfect information is rarely an option. But instinct must be tempered by awareness.

Availability bias is not a flaw of weak leaders; it is a feature of the human brain under pressure. The disciplined leader acknowledges it, tests it, and then decides. On a job-site, momentum matters. So does judgment. The art is not slowing the work; it is slowing the frame through which you interpret it. What comes easily to mind is not always what matters most.

INSIGHT 8 - THE DANGER OF THE SINGLE-ISSUE FRAME

On a construction site, nothing is ever just one thing. Money is tied to schedule. Schedule is tied to manpower. Manpower is tied to morale. Morale is tied to reputation. Yet in the heat of negotiation, complex realities get reduced to a single sentence:

"This is about the change order." No, it isn't. It is about risk, sequencing, cash flow, authority, precedent, and face. The danger of the single-issue frame is not that it simplifies the conversation, it distorts it. And distortion in negotiation is expensive.

The Principle

Negotiations are systems, not single variables.

A seasoned negotiator understands that every dispute sits inside a larger system. When someone frames the conversation around one issue - price, delay, responsibility - it is almost always a surface expression of deeper and connected concerns.

The single-issue frame creates artificial scarcity. If there is only one issue, then one party must win and the other must lose. The conversation collapses into a tug-of-war. But when you widen the frame, options appear.

Consider a mid-rise commercial project running six weeks behind. The electrical subcontractor submits a $280,000 change order for out-of-sequence work caused by late steel deliveries. The general contractor rejects it outright: "We're not paying for your inefficiency."

Now the frame is singular: Is the GC paying $280,000 or not? That frame is lethal.

Because the real system includes:

- Liquidated damages pressure from the owner.
- Cash flow strain on the subcontractor.
- Overtime costs to recover schedule.
- Inspection sequencing with the city.
- Future bid relationships.

If the conversation stays locked on the dollar figure, both sides harden. If it widens to include schedule recovery, shared risk, payment timing, and future opportunities, movement becomes possible. Complex negotiations require dimensional thinking. The more complex the job, the more dangerous the single-issue frame.

The Pitfall

Mistaking the loudest issue for the only issue.

The most common mistake negotiators make is assuming that the issue being argued most forcefully is the core issue. It rarely is.

In construction disputes, money becomes the lightning rod. But money often masks a fear of setting precedent, a concern about looking weak, a breakdown in communication, internal pressure from executives or a need to reassert authority.

When you respond only to the visible issue, you miss the drivers underneath it.

In our example, the GC's project manager may not actually be fighting about $280,000. He may be terrified that approving this change order will trigger five more. Or that his regional manager will question his control of the project. Or that the owner will interpret payment as an admission of fault.

The subcontractor, meanwhile, may not just want money. He may need immediate liquidity to cover payroll because out-of-sequence work destroyed his manpower efficiency. His stance isn't aggression, it's survival. But once both parties lock into the single-issue frame, "Pay it" versus "Not a dime," identity gets attached. Pride enters and positions calcify.

And what could have been a structured business discussion becomes a reputational contest.

Single-issue framing narrows thinking. Narrow thinking increases threat perception. And perceived threat drives escalation.

The Pointer

Expand the frame before you solve the problem.

The practical discipline is simple but powerful: before negotiating the issue, negotiate the frame. When someone says, "This is about the change order," the seasoned negotiator asks: "Is that the only thing this affects?" That question alone widens the aperture.

In the example above, a more effective move by the GC might be: "Let's step back. We've got cost impact, schedule recovery, and owner exposure tied together here. If we solve only one of those, we probably fail. Let's put all of them on the table."

Now the frame shifts from pay vs. deny to how do we manage the combined impact?

Suddenly, creative trades appear:

- Partial payment now, remainder tied to documented acceleration.
- Shared overtime to hit a revised milestone.
- Future bid preference in exchange for compromise.
- Joint presentation to the owner to recover a portion upstream.
- Re-sequencing inspections to reduce cascading delay.

None of those options are visible inside a single-issue frame. Expanding the frame does not mean conceding the issue. It means refusing to negotiate in a distorted box.

The discipline requires emotional control. When attacked with a narrow demand, your instinct will be to counter narrowly. Resist it.

Instead, name the visible issue, identify the connected pressures and invite discussion across all of them. This signals strategic maturity. It reduces defensiveness. And it moves the conversation from confrontation to problem architecture.

The single-issue frame is seductive because it feels efficient. "Let's just solve this one thing." But construction projects are ecosystems. Every decision sends ripple effects through contract language, manpower allocation, risk tolerance, and long-term relationships. When you negotiate one variable in isolation, you often damage another unintentionally.

The seasoned negotiator thinks in systems. They ask: if this moves what else moves? Who else is affected? What precedent does this create? What pressure is driving this demand? They understand that broadening the frame increases both clarity and control.

On a job-site, complexity is not the enemy. Oversimplification is. If you find yourself arguing harder and getting nowhere, pause and examine the frame. Negotiation is rarely about one thing. And when you allow it to become about one thing, you narrow your leverage, your options, and your influence. The danger of the single-issue frame is not that it simplifies the problem. It is that it blinds you to the solution.

INSIGHT 9 – DECOMPOSING THE MESS BEFORE YOU SOLVE IT

Complex negotiations rarely fail because the parties are incapable. They fail because everything is treated as one tangled problem. Money, schedule, authority, safety, reputation, past

grievances, and future leverage all get mashed together into a single emotional knot. When that happens, smart people argue harder instead of thinking clearer.

On a construction project, "the problem" is almost never one problem. It is a mess. And seasoned negotiators know you never solve a mess. You decompose it.

The Principle

Break the big fight into small decisions.

When tension rises on a job-site, the instinct is to solve everything at once. The owner is upset about delays. The GC is blaming weather. The electrical subcontractor says the drawings were incomplete. Change orders are stacking up. Payments are slowing down. Accusations start flying. At that moment, the negotiation is not about schedule. It is about structure.

Decomposition means separating the mess into manageable components before you attempt agreement. At minimum, break it into three categories:

- **Issues** - What specifically must be decided? (Cost? Time extension? Responsibility? Sequencing? Authority?)
- **Actors** - Who actually has decision power? Who influences quietly? Who can veto?
- **Forums** - Which issues must be solved together, and which can be handled separately?

Consider a real-world example: A hospital expansion project is 45 days behind schedule. The owner demands liquidated damages. The general contractor insists the delay is due to late design revisions. The mechanical subcontractor claims it couldn't fabricate on time because approved submittals were delayed.

The first meeting devolves into blame. Everyone argues the whole thing. The seasoned negotiator pauses the chaos and reframes: "Before we debate responsibility, let's separate what needs resolution."

They identify:

1. **Schedule impact** - How many days are truly attributable to design changes?

2. **Cost impact** - What are the actual acceleration costs?
3. **Contract interpretation** - Does the clause allow concurrent delay relief?
4. **Future sequencing** - How do we prevent further slippage?
5. **Relationship preservation** - This team still has 10 months left together.

Once decomposed, the temperature drops. Instead of "You're costing us millions," the conversation becomes, "Let's quantify the schedule impact from Revision 14." Clarity replaces volume.

The Pitfall

Treating emotion as the issue

The biggest mistake negotiators make is assuming that whatever is being argued most loudly is the real issue. It rarely is.

On construction sites, frustration disguises itself as a cost dispute. Ego disguises itself as a contract interpretation issue. Fear of reputational damage disguises itself as a schedule debate.

When everything is argued at once, emotion bleeds across categories. A payment dispute contaminates sequencing decisions. A safety incident contaminates trust. Personal friction contaminates contract analysis.

Without decomposition, parties conflate past grievances with present claims, legal rights with operational realities, and identity threats with financial exposure. The result is escalation.

In the hospital project example, the owner's representative may feel embarrassed in front of hospital leadership. That pressure fuels aggressive posturing. The GC superintendent may feel blamed publicly, triggering defensiveness. The subcontractor may fear being labeled unreliable.

If these emotional drivers are not acknowledged separately from the technical issues, the negotiation becomes positional warfare. People argue harder because they feel unseen.

Decomposition does not ignore emotion. It contains it. By isolating issues, you prevent emotional spillover from infecting every topic.

The Pointer

Negotiate in layers, not in lumps.

Seasoned negotiators move in layers. First, they define the categories, second, they sequence the discussion, and third, they decide what must be bundled and what must not.

In the hospital case, the negotiator might say:

"Let's start with schedule attribution only. No dollar figures yet. Once we agree on days, we'll address cost implications. After that, we'll clarify contract language. Finally, we'll address forward planning." This layering accomplishes three things: it reduces cognitive overload, it lowers emotional intensity and it creates incremental progress.

Small agreements build momentum. Perhaps the parties agree that 18 of the 45 days were caused by design revisions. That partial clarity changes the tone of the room. Now the argument is more narrow, less personal and more factual.

Then cost can be discussed within that defined frame.

Not all issues should be solved together. Bundling everything increases complexity and resistance. Some issues are operational and can be delegated to field teams. Others are contractual and require executive-level attention.

Layering also helps identify silent actors. Maybe the hospital's legal counsel has veto power over any liquidated damages waiver. Maybe the project executive - not the superintendent - must approve acceleration costs.

If the wrong people are negotiating the wrong layer, progress stalls. Decomposition ensures the right decision-makers are engaged at the right stage.

Decomposing the mess is not about slowing progress. It is about enabling it. Complex negotiations feel urgent. Pressure tempts you to "just work it out." But without structure, urgency becomes chaos. Remember, everything connects - cost, time, safety, reputation, and performance history. If you treat the negotiation as a single monolithic problem, you will trigger defensiveness and confusion.

But when you separate what is factual from what is emotional, what is contractual from what is operational and what is urgent from what is important, you create clarity and clarity creates leverage.

The seasoned negotiator understands this truth: You cannot solve complexity by adding force. You solve it by adding structure.

INSIGHT 10 – NEGOTIATING IN LAYERS, NOT ALL AT ONCE

Complex negotiations collapse when everything is treated as one big argument.

On a construction project, disputes rarely involve just one issue. A delay claim may involve schedule, cost, manpower, sequencing, authority, reputation, and future work opportunities. Yet the instinct in tense moments is to "clear the air" and tackle it all in one meeting. That instinct is understandable - and destructive.

Seasoned negotiators work differently. They negotiate in layers.

The Principle

Decompose the mess before you try to solve it.

Layered negotiation begins with disciplined separation. Before debating solutions, you break the problem into distinct components.

Layered negotiation begins with disciplined separation. Before debating solutions, you break the problem into distinct components. When everything is blended together, emotion from one issue contaminates all the others.

A perceived insult about workmanship suddenly poisons discussion about change order pricing. A schedule disagreement morphs into a challenge to someone's competence. Layering restores clarity.

- First layer: establish the factual schedule baseline.
- Second layer: identify responsibility for specific delay events.
- Third layer: quantify cost impacts.
- Fourth layer: address forward-looking mitigation and relationship repair

Each layer builds on the previous one. Each layer has its own conversation, sometimes its own meeting, and sometimes its own participants. Layering slows the conversation down - but it speeds the resolution up.

The Pitfall

Trying to win the whole war in one meeting.

The common mistake is escalation by accumulation. Imagine this scenario:

A general contractor and a mechanical subcontractor are arguing over a 21-day delay. The subcontractor claims late steel deliveries disrupted installation sequencing. The GC insists the subcontractor under-staffed the job. The owner is pressing the GC for liquidated damages.

They schedule a "global resolution meeting." Within 20 minutes:

- The scheduler is arguing critical path logic.
- The project manager is debating manpower curves.
- The superintendent is defending field performance.
- The accounting department is disputing cost backup.
- The company principal is warning about future bid opportunities.

Five separate disputes are happening simultaneously. Voices rise. Documents are waved in the air. Accusations spill across issues: "You've been slow since day one," "Well you changed the sequence three times." "You're just trying to back-charge us."

By lunch, no one remembers what the original 21 days actually consisted of. The negotiation has become a referendum on competence, integrity, and power. When you negotiate everything at once, you multiply emotional risk. Every disagreement feels existential. Every concession feels like surrender and the meeting ends with more entrenchment than progress.

The Pointer

Sequence the negotiation deliberately - the hidden advantage of layers.

Layered negotiation is not passive. It is strategically sequenced.

In the same scenario, a seasoned negotiator would intervene early: "Let's not solve everything today. First, let's agree on the timeline."

Layer One: Establish Shared Facts: The parties jointly review the schedule updates and daily reports. They agree on what physically occurred: steel arrived on these dates; manpower levels were these numbers; inspections happened on these days. No blame yet. Just chronology and agreement on facts reduces later distortion.

Layer Two: Assign causation event by event. Instead of debating "Who caused the delay?" they analyze specific time blocks:

- Days 1-6: confirmed late steel delivery.
- Days 7-12: stacking trades in mechanical areas.
- Days 13-21: reduced manpower compared to bid loading.

Now responsibility is distributed across time segments, not argued as a single lump accusation.

Layer Three: Quantify impact. Only after causation is separated do they evaluate cost:

- Extended field overhead.
- Idle labor.
- Acceleration costs.

By this stage, emotional intensity has already dropped because the discussion is anchored to defined segments rather than personal attacks.

Layer Four: Future protection - Finally, address forward-looking protection:

- Adjusted manpower commitments.
- Updated sequencing coordination.
- Escalation protocol if materials slip again.

Notice what did not happen: no one tried to settle money before facts were clarified. No one debated reputation while schedule logic was unresolved. Layering creates psychological safety. People defend less when they are not defending everything at once.

Negotiating in layers also protects relationships. On job sites, parties must continue working together long after the dispute is resolved. When you fight on all fronts simultaneously, you damage future cooperation.

Layered negotiation allows partial agreements. Even in conflict, you can say: "we agree on the timeline, we agree steel was late but we disagree about manpower." Partial agreement builds momentum and preserves dignity.

It also exposes leverage accurately. If 6 of 21 days are clearly excusable, then 15 days remain open for real negotiation. The battlefield shrinks to its legitimate size.

Layered negotiation requires restraint. You must resist:

- The urge to correct every accusation immediately.
- The temptation to introduce new grievances mid-discussion.
- The impulse to demand global settlement before clarity exists.

Instead, you guide the conversation with sequencing language: "One issue at a time." "Let's finish this layer before moving to cost." "We'll get to that after we settle the timeline." This is not avoidance, it is control.

Remember, complex disputes feel urgent and overwhelming. That pressure tempts leaders to compress everything into one high-stakes confrontation. But complexity cannot be bullied into simplicity. Break the problem apart, sequence the issues, clarify facts before blame, and negotiate in layers, not all at once.

CHAPTER TWO

HARD BARGAINING WITHOUT ESCALATION

"Manufactured urgency is one of the oldest tactics in negotiation and one of the most misunderstood."

INSIGHT 11 - WHAT HARD BARGAINING REALLY IS

There is a myth that hard bargaining is about force.

It conjures images of slammed folders, sharp ultimatums, and someone declaring, “That’s my final offer.” In some circles, being labeled a “hard negotiator” is a badge of honor. In others, it’s a warning.

Skilled negotiators who bargain hard do so deliberately. They remain calm, controlled, and precise, using firmness to protect critical interests while avoiding unnecessary escalation. Hard bargaining has very little to do with volume, intimidation, or theatrics.

It is about disciplined boundaries. The strength of hard bargaining is not in hostility, but in the negotiator’s ability to signal seriousness, maintain composure under pressure, and ensure the other side understands that some issues are not flexible.

The Principle

Hard bargaining is about protecting value, not projecting power.

Truly, hard bargaining is the disciplined protection of value - your time, your margin, your risk exposure, and your reputation. It is not about overpowering the other side. It is about refusing to erode what matters.

A seasoned negotiator understands that every agreement allocates four things: money, risk, control, and face. Hard bargaining means you are unwilling to casually give away any of them.

It sounds like this:

- "That risk allocation doesn't work for us."
- "We're prepared to move forward at this number, but not below it."
- "If that clause stays, the price changes." Notice the tone: calm, direct, unembellished.

Hard bargaining is quiet. It does not require performance. It does not require hostility. It requires clarity about where your line is - and the composure to hold it. When done well, it actually reduces conflict. The other side may not like your position, but they understand it. Clear boundaries create predictable behavior. Predictable behavior creates stability and stability builds credibility. Hard bargaining is credibility under pressure.

The Pitfall

Turning the negotiation into a test of will.

The most common mistake is confusing firmness with dominance. When negotiators feel pressure, they often escalate tone. They sharpen language. They repeat "non-negotiable" before they have fully assessed their own flexibility.

Then the conversation shifts from substance to ego. Now it is no longer about solving a problem. It is about who blinks first. This is dangerous for three reasons.

1. First, ego-based bargaining blinds you to information. When you focus on "winning," you stop listening. And when you stop listening, you miss leverage.
2. Second, it triggers defensiveness. The other side digs in - not because your terms are unreasonable, but because backing down feels like humiliation.
3. Third, it traps you. Once you posture as immovable, you lose room to maneuver. If you later discover a smarter path, you cannot pivot without appearing weak.

Hard bargaining is not rigidity. It is selective inflexibility.

Another subtle pitfall is false toughness - declaring a line you are not prepared to enforce. If you threaten to walk and then stay, you have permanently weakened your credibility. Nothing erodes negotiating power faster than an empty ultimatum.

Hard bargaining requires the willingness to endure impasse. If you cannot tolerate the possibility of no deal, you are not bargaining hard. You are bargaining anxiously. And anxiety makes concessions.

The Pointer

Separate your line from your identity.

The most effective hard bargainers detach their self-worth from the outcome. They do not need to "win." They need to protect defined interests.

Before entering any serious negotiation, answer three questions:

1. What must this agreement accomplish?
2. What is the maximum exposure I will accept?

3. What will I do if we do not reach agreement?

Then write the answers down: numbers, conditions and triggers.

Clarity reduces emotional volatility.

In the room, apply three Disciplined Behaviors:

1. State your boundary once, clearly. “We can proceed at $X under these terms.” Do not over-explain. Over-explanation signals discomfort.
2. When challenged, restate without escalation. “I understand the concern but that’s still where we are.” Calm repetition communicates seriousness.
3. Trade, don’t cave. If you move, move conditionally. “If delivery shifts to Q3, we can revisit pricing.” “If indemnity language changes, we can adjust scope.” Movement tied to structure preserves strength.

And perhaps most importantly, learn to tolerate silence. After stating your position, stop talking.

Silence is pressure. Many negotiators fill silence with concessions because they mistake discomfort for danger. The seasoned negotiator knows that silence is simply space where the other side recalculates. Hard bargaining is often nothing more than holding steady while others grow uncomfortable.

It is not cruelty, stubbornness or hostility. It is disciplined clarity about value.

It is the ability to say “no” without anger. It is the ability to say “yes” without regret and the ability to walk away without theatrics. Hard bargaining protects what matters while leaving the relationship intact.

In long-term professional relationships with clients, vendors, partners, and colleagues, reputation compounds. The negotiator known for clear boundaries and consistent behavior earns something more powerful than fear. They earn respect. And respect is leverage that does not expire.

Hard bargaining, properly understood, is not about being the toughest person in the room. It is about being the most internally anchored. The person who knows their line and can hold it calmly rarely has to raise their voice to be taken seriously.

INSIGHT 12 - ANCHORS, THREATS, AND ARTIFICIAL DEADLINES

Negotiation is rarely just a discussion of terms. It is a contest over perception. And three of the most common tools used to shape perception are anchors, threats, and artificial deadlines. They are powerful. They are often manipulative. And they are everywhere.

An anchor is an opening position, often extreme and designed to shape the range of discussions that follow. Once a number, demand or position is placed on the table, it tends to frame the entire conversation.

Threats are attempts to force movement through intimidation or suggestion of negative consequences. They may be explicit or implied. Artificial deadlines are designed to shorten your thinking time. The seasoned negotiator does not panic when these tools appear. He studies them.

The Principle

Control the Frame, Not the Reaction.

Anchors, threats, and deadlines are not arguments. They are pressure devices. Their purpose is not to persuade you logically but to define reality before you speak. A threat attempts to narrow your options through fear. An artificial deadline attempts to rush you into agreement before you can analyze. The principle is simple: pressure only works when you react to it emotionally rather than strategically.

The first number on the table does not become true simply because it was spoken first. A threat does not become credible because it sounds forceful. A deadline does not become binding because someone says, "This offer expires today."

Inexperienced negotiators treat these tactics as facts. Experienced negotiators treat them as signals. An aggressive anchor signals the other side is trying to frame the zone of discussion. A threat signals insecurity or lack of alternatives. A sudden deadline signals leverage anxiety.

The goal is not to counterattack immediately. The goal is to regain time and space. Time is oxygen in negotiation. Whoever feels rushed is rarely thinking clearly. The disciplined negotiator slows the room down. He does not argue the anchor. He questions the assumptions behind it. He does not react to the threat. He evaluates its credibility. He does not surrender to the deadline. He tests its reality. Control the frame, not the reaction.

The Pitfall

Confusing urgency with importance.

The most common mistake negotiators make is allowing urgency to distort judgment.

An extreme anchor creates emotional shock. You feel offended or defensive. And in that emotional response, you inadvertently legitimize the number by negotiating against it.

A threat creates anxiety. You imagine worst-case scenarios and begin conceding to avoid them.

An artificial deadline creates fear of loss. You focus on not missing the deal rather than evaluating whether it is the right deal.

In construction negotiations, this dynamic is common. A subcontractor submits a change order with an inflated price, claiming material costs are "skyrocketing." The number is far above expectation. The project manager reacts by immediately countering with a lower number - without first dissecting labor, material, markup, and schedule impacts. The anchor has already shaped the battlefield.

Or consider a general contractor who says, "If we don't sign this by Friday, I'll award it to another bidder." The implied threat triggers fear of losing the project. The artificial deadline creates compression. The firm signs without clarifying scope exclusions.

Months later, the disputes begin. The pitfall is not that anchors, threats, and deadlines exist. They always will. The pitfall is reacting to pressure instead of diagnosing it. Urgency does not equal importance, volume does not equal leverage and deadlines do not equal inevitability.

When you confuse speed with wisdom, you negotiate against yourself.

The Pointer

Slow it down, break it apart, test it.

There are three moves that neutralize pressure tactics.

1. Slow the tempo. When confronted with an extreme anchor or looming deadline, resist the urge to respond immediately. Say, "Help me understand how you arrived at that figure." Or, "Let's walk through the components." Slowing down will signal steadiness. It also forces the other party to justify their frame.
2. Break the issue into pieces. Anchors thrive in vagueness. Break the number into labor, materials, equipment, risk allocation, and contingency. Threats weaken when examined against contractual language and practical consequences. Deadlines often dissolve when you ask what specifically changes after the stated date. Artificial deadlines frequently reveal themselves when calmly probed. "What happens Monday that doesn't happen Friday?" is a powerful question.
3. Test credibility quietly. If someone threatens to walk away, assess their alternatives. Do they truly have another bidder? Would switching contractors delay the schedule? Would termination trigger litigation costs? Most threats are costlier to execute than to state. Testing credibility is not confrontation. It is evaluation.

In a construction bid negotiation, imagine a developer anchors aggressively low, stating, "This is the final number, and we need it signed by 5 p.m." The seasoned contractor does not argue emotionally. He responds: "We want to make this work. Let's review scope alignment to ensure we're comparing the same deliverables. If timing is critical, let's outline what decisions are dependent on today and what can move into a follow-up session."

The tempo shifts. The emotional pressure eases. Space returns to the room. Often, the "final" number moves. The "firm" deadline extends. Not because you fought harder - but because you refused to be rushed.

Anchors, threats, and artificial deadlines are tools of compression. They attempt to shrink your thinking window. The disciplined negotiator expands it. He understands that pressure is part of the theater of negotiation. But he does not confuse theater with reality.

He does not flinch at the first number, he does not concede at the first threat, he does not sign at the first clock. He slows, he dissects, he tests and in doing so, he negotiates from clarity rather than fear.

INSIGHT 13 - RECOGNIZING MANUFACTURED URGENCY

There is a particular tone that enters a negotiation when urgency is invoked. "We need this signed today." "If this isn't resolved by 3:00pm, the deal is off." "Corporate needs an answer right now."

Urgency feels powerful because time pressure compresses thinking. It narrows options, elevates emotion, and forces movement. But not all urgency is real. Some of it is engineered. Manufactured urgency is one of the oldest pressure tactics in negotiation and one of the most misunderstood.

The seasoned negotiator does not automatically resist urgency.

He evaluates it.

The Principle

Time pressure is a tool, not a fact.

Deadlines are often presented as immovable realities. In truth, many are strategic devices designed to accelerate commitment before analysis can catch up. Manufactured urgency works because it hijacks three human tendencies: fear of missing out, appearing indecisive and assuming someone else's timeline must be more informed than ours.

When urgency appears, the untrained negotiator reacts to the clock. The experienced negotiator interrogates the clock.

They ask:

- What happens if this deadline passes?
- Who imposed it?
- What cost does the other side incur if it slips?
- Is this tied to an external event or internal convenience?

Real urgency usually has external anchors, financing windows, regulatory cutoffs, market shifts, weather events, or contractual milestones. Manufactured urgency tends to revolve around internal preferences, quarterly optics, or vague threats of lost opportunity.

Time pressure is leverage. But leverage only works if you accept it as binding. The disciplined negotiator slows down before speeding up. They understand that agreeing under artificial compression often creates larger problems later, unexamined risks, incomplete terms, and misunderstood expectations.

The principle is simple: urgency must be verified before it is obeyed.

The Pitfall

Confusing movement with progress.

Manufactured urgency creates motion. But motion is not the same as resolution. Under time pressure, negotiators tend to:

- Concede too quickly to "keep things moving."
- Skip clarification to avoid appearing obstructive.
- Agree to ambiguous language with the promise of "cleaning it up later."
- Trade long-term value for short-term relief.

The psychological relief of removing pressure can feel like a win.

It is not.

One of the most common errors is believing that speed signals strength. In reality, speed often signals anxiety. When someone rushes you, it is frequently because delay weakens their position more than yours. Manufactured urgency exploits that social pressure:

"Everyone else has agreed. "You're the last signature."

"We've already announced this internally."

These phrases are designed to isolate you. The danger is not that you will lose the deal. The danger is that you will accept terms you would never accept under normal conditions simply to relieve the discomfort of time compression.

Manufactured urgency makes negotiators reactive. And reactive negotiators trade leverage for speed.

The Pointer

Slow the tempo without escalating the tension.

Recognizing manufactured urgency is only half the battle. Responding to it skillfully is where discipline shows. The goal is not to accuse the other side of manipulation. The goal is to normalize due diligence. There are several effective moves:

1. Separate the decision from the deadline - Acknowledge the timeline without committing to it. "I understand the importance of your timeline but to make a responsible decision, I need clarity on a few points." This reframes caution as professionalism, not resistance.
2. Ask calibrated questions. Instead of rejecting the deadline, explore it. "What specifically changes if this is decided tomorrow instead of today?" "Who is impacted if we extend these issues 48 hours?" Real urgency will produce concrete answers. Manufactured urgency often produces vague ones.
3. Introduce process transparency. "I need to walk this through legal and operations before committing." This shifts the dynamic from personal hesitation to institutional necessity.
4. Control your own tempo. Silence is powerful under time pressure. So is measured pacing. When the other side accelerates, slow your speech. Slow your movements. Slowness communicates steadiness. Steadiness resists compression.
5. Be willing to let the clock expire. The ultimate test of manufactured urgency is whether the opportunity truly disappears. Frequently, it does not. Deadlines that dissolve quietly were never structural to begin with.

The seasoned negotiator understands that leverage shifts as time passes. If someone pushes for immediate resolution, it often means delay strengthens your position.

Recognizing manufactured urgency is not about stubbornness. It is about clarity. Sometimes urgency is real. Storms arrive. Markets close. Financing windows expire. When urgency is legitimate, decisive action is strength. But when urgency is manufactured, patience is strength.

The disciplined negotiator asks is this deadline tied to reality or strategy? Is this pressure structural or tactical? Negotiation is not won by the fastest mover. It is won by the clearest thinker. The skilled negotiator decides which it will be.

INSIGHT 14 - RESPONDING WITHOUT REACTING

There is a moment in every negotiation when the temperature rises. A number is thrown on the table that feels insulting. A comment is made that questions your competence. A deadline appears that smells artificial. The room tightens. Your jaw sets. Your voice wants to sharpen.

In that moment, the negotiation is no longer about the issue on the table. It is about you.

Seasoned negotiators understand something that less experienced ones do not: the most expensive decisions are often made in the first five emotional seconds of a conversation. The ability to respond without reacting is not a personality trait. It is a discipline. And it is decisive.

The Principle

Reaction is instinct; response is strategy.

Reaction is immediate, emotional, and defensive. It is driven by ego, fear, surprise, or anger. Reaction narrows your thinking. It turns complex negotiations into binary contests. It escalates. Response, on the other hand, is intentional. It is measured. It creates space between stimulus and decision. That space is where strategy lives.

When someone says, "That price is ridiculous," a reaction sounds like, "Then maybe you should find someone else." A response sounds like, "Help me understand what feels unreasonable."

The difference is subtle in language but enormous in impact. Reaction protects pride, response protects leverage, reaction feels powerful in the moment but response builds power over time.

Emotional surges are not signs of weakness. They are signals that something matters. But if you allow emotion to dictate your timing and tone, you surrender control of the negotiation environment. Once escalation begins, both sides start arguing positions more aggressively, and the original interests become harder to reach.

The disciplined negotiator understands that silence is often stronger than rebuttal. A pause can calm a room more effectively than a counterattack. Then, asking a clarifying question can redirect tension without conceding ground.

Responding without reacting is not passive. It is self-management in search of a strategic advantage.

The Pitfall

Confusing speed with strength.

Many professionals equate quick responses with competence. They believe that hesitating looks weak or unprepared. So, when challenged, they fire back immediately and this is where they lose control. In tense moments, the nervous system activates before rational analysis. Words come faster than thought. Tone sharpens. The other party mirrors that energy. Escalation becomes mutual and automatic.

The pitfall is assuming that you must defend instantly or risk losing credibility.

In reality, instant defense often signals insecurity. It tells the other side they have touched something sensitive. They press harder.

Another common mistake is overcorrecting, trying so hard not to react that you suppress emotion entirely. Suppression is not discipline. It leaks through body language, clipped responses, or delayed resentment that resurfaces later. The goal is not emotional absence. It is emotional regulation.

There is also a tactical risk. Reactive statements often lock you into positions you later regret. You make commitments or threats that shrink your flexibility. You turn a negotiable issue into a matter of principle because you spoke from pride rather than strategy. And pride is expensive.

The Pointer

Build the pause.

The skill of responding without reacting can be trained. It begins with one simple habit: build the pause. When confronted with a provocative statement:

1. Breathe before you speak. A single controlled breath interrupts the automatic stress response.
2. Lower your voice instead of raising it. Tone often resets the room faster than content.
3. Ask a question before making a counterpoint. Questions shift you from defense to discovery.
4. Name the tension neutrally. "It sounds like there's frustration around the schedule." Naming emotion reduces its intensity.

The pause does three powerful things.

1. First, it signals composure. Composure changes how others assess your authority. Calm negotiators are perceived as more confident and more prepared.
2. Second, it buys cognitive time. You regain access to strategic thinking rather than operating from impulse.
3. Third, it often causes the other party to fill the silence, revealing more information than they intended.

Another practical technique is to separate identity from issue. When someone criticizes your proposal, resist hearing it as criticism of you. Reframe internally: "This is about the numbers, not my competence." That mental distinction preserves clarity.

Finally, decide in advance how you will handle provocation. Pre-commitment reduces emotional surprise. If you expect anchoring tactics, threats, or sharp language, they will not destabilize you when they arrive.

The strongest negotiators are not those who never feel

anger or pressure. They are those who refuse to let those feelings dictate their timing. Responding without reacting is not about being calm for its own sake. It is about maintaining control of the tempo, tone, and trajectory of the negotiation. When you master the pause, you shift the balance of power. The room begins to move at your pace. Escalation slows. Clarity increases. Options reappear.

And in high-stakes negotiations, that space - those few measured seconds between stimulus and response - can be the difference between a costly concession and a durable agreement.

INSIGHT 15 – NAMING TENSION WITHOUT LIGHTING IT

Tension is inevitable in negotiation. The question is not whether it will appear, but whether you will handle it skillfully or accidentally ignite it.

Most negotiators fear tension. They either ignore it, hoping it will pass, or confront it bluntly, triggering defensiveness. Both reactions misunderstand what tension is.

Tension is information. It tells you where identity feels threatened, where risk feels high, where trust feels thin. The seasoned negotiator does not suppress tension and does not inflame it. They name it - carefully.

This is the difference between managing heat and creating fire.

The Principle

Tension named neutrally loses its volatility.

When tension rises, the room changes. Voices sharpen. Silence hardens. Postures stiffen. People stop exploring and start protecting.

If you pretend not to see it, it intensifies beneath the surface. If you accuse someone of causing it, you escalate it. The principle is simple: Name the tension without assigning blame, motive, or judgment.

There is a world of difference between: "You're getting defensive," and "It feels like this issue carries a lot of weight for both sides." The first statement personalizes. The second contextualizes.

Neutral naming accomplishes three things:

1. It makes the implicit explicit. Everyone feels the tension, but no one has acknowledged it. Once named, it becomes discussable rather than combustible.
2. It reduces misinterpretation. Silence in tense moments is often read as hostility. Naming tension reframes it as pressure rather than malice.
3. It lowers the temperature. When someone calmly identifies what is happening in the room, the emotional charge decreases. People feel seen without feeling attacked.

Effective naming uses language like:

- "It seems this point is landing hard."
- "There's clearly concern around this."
- "I sense we may be reacting to more than just the numbers."

Notice what these phrases avoid: they do not assign intent, they do not diagnose personality, and they do not accuse.

They illuminate without igniting.

The moment tension is acknowledged neutrally, it often softens.

The room breathes again. Conversation resumes.

The Pitfall

Mistaking directness for skill.

Many negotiators pride themselves on "calling it like it is." They believe bluntness equals strength. But naming tension is not the same as calling someone out.

The common mistake is moving from observation to accusation. Instead of: "There's hesitation around this timeline,"

They say: "You're stalling."

Instead of: "This proposal seems to create risk concerns," They say: "You don't trust us."

These statements light matches because they attribute motive. The human brain reacts to perceived accusations as a threat. Once a threat enters the room, problem-solving exits.

Another pitfall is over-intellectualizing emotion:

- "Your reaction suggests cognitive dissonance."
- "You're projecting."
- These may sound analytical, but they feel condescending. Nothing inflames tension faster than feeling analyzed.
- The final mistake is weaponized empathy:
- "I can see you're upset."

When said with the wrong tone, this doesn't calm, it patronizes.

Naming tension without lighting it requires restraint. The goal is not to win the emotional moment. The goal is to stabilize the conversation. If your words increase self-protection in the other party, you've added oxygen to the fire.

The Pointer

Describe the weather, not the person.

A practical technique is this: describe the weather in the room, not the personality of the people in it. Weather language externalizes tension. It treats it as a shared condition rather than a personal flaw.

Examples:

- "This feels like a high-stakes decision."
- "There's some friction here."
- "This topic carries a lot of history."

Notice the framing. The tension exists in the situation, not in the character of the individuals.

Another powerful pointer: Slow your pace when naming tension. Speed escalates. Calm tempo regulates. If your voice remains even and measured, your naming functions as a stabilizer rather than a spark.

You can also pair naming with invitation:

- "It seems like there's concern around the risk allocation. What's most important for you to feel comfortable here?"
- "This feels like a sticking point. Can we unpack what's underneath it?"

The invitation shifts the energy from confrontation to exploration.

Finally, understand timing. Naming tension too early can create self-consciousness. Naming it too late can allow it to calcify. The skill lies in sensing when the room has shifted - when curiosity has given way to rigidity. That is the moment to step in, and step in lightly. Tension is not a problem to eliminate. It is a signal that something meaningful is at stake.

The seasoned negotiator does not rush to extinguish it or overpower it. They acknowledge it with precision. They speak in language that clarifies rather than condemns. They regulate their own tone before attempting to regulate the room.

When you name tension without lighting it, you demonstrate something rare: emotional steadiness under pressure and steadiness is contagious.

In high-stakes negotiation, the calmest person often shapes the outcome, not because they speak the loudest, but because they manage the heat without feeding the flame.

INSIGHT 16 - REFRAMING ACCUSATIONS INTO ISSUES

Accusations are negotiations in disguise. They rarely appear as questions. They show up as sharp sentences, loaded with blame:

- "You dropped the ball."
- "You're trying to bury us."
- "You don't care about this project."

The inexperienced negotiator hears attack and responds with defense. The seasoned negotiator hears heat and looks for structure.

The question, how do we convert accusations into negotiable issues?

The Principle

Every accusation contains a hidden issue.

An accusation is not a strategy. It is a signal. It tells you where someone feels harmed, threatened, or disadvantaged.

When a subcontractor says, "You're squeezing us dry," the literal statement is an attack on motive. But underneath it may be an issue of cash flow, risk allocation, or perceived unfairness in scope changes.

When an owner says, "Your team is incompetent," the hidden issue is rarely intelligence. It is schedule reliability, communication gaps, or quality control.

Accusations collapse multiple concerns into one emotionally charged statement. They blur facts, feelings, and fear into a single line. If you respond to the accusation itself - arguing about intent, defending competence, counterattacking - you stay trapped at the surface level.

Reframing means translating.

"You're trying to bury us" becomes: "It sounds like you're concerned about the cost exposure on these change orders."

"You don't care about the schedule" becomes: "It sounds like we're not aligned on the timeline risk here."

Notice what happens. The emotional charge drops. The focus shifts from character to condition. From motive to mechanism. From blame to structure.

The principle is simple: Behind every accusation is an issue worth naming. When you name the issue clearly and calmly, you move the conversation back into the realm of problem-solving.

The Pitfall

Fighting the accusation instead of addressing the issue.

The most common mistake is reflexive defense. Someone says, "You're sandbagging us."

You respond, "That's ridiculous. We've been transparent from day one."

Now you are arguing about integrity. And integrity debates are unwinnable in the moment. The more you defend, the more the other side feels unheard. Then the accusation intensifies. Defense feels natural because accusations feel personal. But reacting personally is precisely what escalates the conflict.

A second pitfall is counter-accusation. "You're accusing us of delays? Your crew was late for three weeks."

This shifts the negotiation into a courtroom. Each side compiles evidence. Each side prosecutes. Resolution becomes secondary to vindication.

A third pitfall is ignoring the accusation altogether - moving on as if it was never said. This leaves emotional heat unaddressed. The issue resurfaces later, often louder.

The deeper mistake in all three responses is the same: staying at the level of blame. Blame is sticky. Issues are movable.

If you fight the accusation, you strengthen it. If you counterattack, you widen the rift. If you ignore it, you postpone the explosion.

Reframing is the disciplined alternative.

The Pointer

Translate emotion into structure in real time.

Reframing is not passive. It requires composure and clarity. The moment you hear an accusation, slow your response. Your first job is not to rebut. It is to decode.

Ask yourself silently:

- What concrete concern is hiding inside this statement?
- Is this about money, schedule, authority, risk, respect, or communication?
- What decision or condition is actually in dispute? Then respond with translation language:
- "It sounds like..."
- "What I'm hearing is..."
- "Let's separate the concern from the language..."

For example: Accusation: "You're nickel-and-diming every change."

Reframe: "It sounds like the volume and pricing of change orders feel unpredictable. Let's look at how we're scoping and approving them."

Accusation: "You set us up to fail."

Reframe: "Are you concerned that the sequencing created constraints your team couldn't manage?"

You are not agreeing with the accusation. You are extracting the issue. Two things happen when you do this well. First, the other party often softens. When someone feels understood, their tone shifts - even if they still disagree. Second, you regain control of the structure. The conversation moves from who is wrong to what needs adjustment.

If the other side says, "That's not what I meant," that is not failure.

It is clarification. You have invited precision instead of perpetuating heat. Another powerful move is to write the issue down in visible form during a meeting:

Issue 1: Change order pricing predictability.

Issue 2: Sequencing constraints affecting productivity.

Writing converts accusation into agenda. Once it is on the board, it is no longer a weapon; it is a work item.

Finally, maintain neutral language. Tone matters as much as wording. Reframing delivered with sarcasm will inflame rather than calm. Reframing delivered steadily signals leadership. Accusations are inevitable in high-stakes environments. Pressure compresses language. Fear sharpens tone. When money, reputation, and timelines are involved, people speak in absolutes.

The seasoned negotiator does not get trapped in the absolutes. They understand that accusations are clumsy containers for legitimate concerns. Reframing does not mean tolerating abuse. It means refusing to negotiate at the level of personal attack. It means elevating the conversation back to substance.

The shift is subtle but powerful:

- From "You're incompetent." To "We need a clearer quality control process."
- From "You don't care." To "We are misaligned on priorities."
- From "You're trying to win at our expense." To "We need to rebalance risk in this agreement."

In the end, negotiations do not collapse because of harsh words. They collapse because harsh words are left untranslated. When you master the discipline of reframing accusations into issues, you transform conflict from confrontation into construction.

And construction – whether of buildings or agreements – always begins with structure.

INSIGHT 17 - SEPARATING POSITIONS FROM INTERESTS

In negotiation, most people argue positions. Seasoned negotiators explore interests. The difference sounds subtle. In practice, it determines whether conversations harden into standoffs

or evolve into solutions. A position is what someone says they want. An interest is why they want it.

When you negotiate at the level of position, the conversation narrows. When you negotiate at the level of interest, the conversation opens.

This insight is about learning to recognize the difference - and having the discipline to stay in the deeper layer.

The Principle

Positions are the surface; Interests are the structure beneath.

A position is concrete and visible.

- "We need $250,000."
- "We can't extend the schedule."
- "That's not acceptable."
- "This is non-negotiable."

Positions feel solid. They are easy to state and easy to defend. But they are often the visible tip of something much more important underneath.

Interests are the drivers behind the position:

- Security
- Predictability
- Reputation
- Cash flow
- Authority
- Risk allocation
- Identity
- Fairness

When someone says, "We need $250,000," the interest may be:

- Covering unexpected cost exposure.
- Avoiding a quarterly loss.
- Protecting internal credibility.
- Managing debt covenants.

The number is the position. The protection is the interest. If you attack the number, you harden the defense.

If you explore the protection, you create options. The most important shift in strategic negotiation is this: positions compete; interests can align.

Two sides can have opposing positions and still share compatible interests.

A contractor says, "We need a 90-day extension." An owner says, "No extensions."

On the surface there is deadlock.

Underneath:

- The Contractor interest is avoiding liquidated damages and protecting workforce stability.
- The Owner interest is to open the facility before peak season and satisfy the financing conditions.
- Now the conversation can move:
- Can partial occupancy solve timing pressure?
- Can liquidated damages be structured differently?
- Can workforce sequencing protect both side Once interests are visible, creativity becomes possible.

The Pitfall

Arguing the position harder.

The natural mistake is to argue the position more forcefully. When someone resists your demand, instinct says justify it better. Add spreadsheets, add case law, then add volume.

But when both sides defend positions, negotiation turns into a comparison of stubbornness. This is the trap of surface bargaining. Each side becomes more invested in defending what was said than in examining why it was said. And something subtle happens. Ego fuses with position and now backing away feels like losing.

In construction disputes, this is especially common. A subcontractor says, "We're owed full compensation for delay." The general contractor says, "The contract doesn't allow that." Each side cites language. Each side reinforces entitlement.

Meanwhile, the real interests may be:

- Subcontractor - survival cash flow.
- GC - avoiding precedent with other trades.
- Owner - keeping the project out of litigation.

None of those interests are addressed by arguing clauses alone.

Another version of this pitfall is assuming the first position expressed is the real issue. It rarely is. Early positions are often protective. They are shields. If you react to the shield instead of exploring what it protects, the conversation becomes defensive from the start.

The more threatened someone feels, the more rigid their position becomes. And rigidity is often fear in disguise.

The Pointer

Get curious before you get creative.

Instead of countering a position, the seasoned negotiator will ask structured curiosity questions:

- "Help me understand what's driving that number."
- "What risk are you trying to protect against?"
- "If we solved the timing issue, would the dollar issue feel different?"
- "What would have to be true for this to work for you?"

Notice what these questions do. They do not challenge the position. They explore the interest behind it.

This does three powerful things:

1. It lowers defensiveness.
2. It reveals flexibility that was not visible at the surface.
3. It shifts the tone from adversarial to diagnostic.

Think of it as moving from debate to investigation. You are not trying to win the argument. You are trying to understand the architecture underneath it. Once interests are clear, you can begin option-building. If the interest is cash flow, maybe structure changes help.

If the interest is risk exposure, maybe insurance adjustments solve it. If the interest is reputation, maybe communication agreements matter more than dollars. You cannot build smart options until you understand the load-bearing beams.

One more subtle pointer: separate your own interests from your stated position. Often, we defend our position because we have not clarified our own deeper drivers.

Ask yourself:

- What am I really trying to protect?
- Is this number essential, or is the outcome essential?
- What would satisfy my interest even if the position changes?

Flexibility at the interest level creates leverage at the outcome level. When negotiations stall, explore if your interests are incompatible or a result of positions colliding. Positions are easy to argue. Interests require inquiry. Positions are rigid statements. Interests are human concerns.

If you discipline yourself to listen past the first demand, to ask before countering, and to diagnose before designing, you will find that many "impossible" negotiations are simply conversations that never moved beneath the surface.

Separate positions from interests. When you do, you stop negotiating over statements and start negotiating over solutions.

INSIGHT 18 - HOLDING THE LINE WHEN VOICES RISE

There is a moment in certain negotiations when the temperature changes.

Voices sharpen. Interruptions multiply. Someone leans forward, not to persuade but to overpower. The volume rises in proportion to the anxiety in the room. And in that moment, many negotiators make a silent, fateful choice: match the intensity or surrender to it.

Neither works. Holding the line when voices rise is not about dominance. It is about discipline. It is the art of staying steady when others lose theirs.

The Principle

Emotional escalation is a test of structure, not strength.

When volume increases, structure decreases. People raise their voices when they feel unheard, threatened, cornered, or losing control. Noise is often an attempt to regain leverage. It is less about the content of the disagreement and more about the perceived imbalance of power, respect, or security.

The seasoned negotiator understands something critical: escalation is an invitation. It invites you to abandon process and engage in combat. It invites you to defend ego instead of clarify issues. It invites you to react.

Holding the line means refusing that invitation. This does not require silence or passivity. It requires structure. When voices rise, structure must rise with them. The more emotional the room becomes, the more procedural you become. Instead of arguing content, you stabilize the container. You slow the pace. You lower your volume. You narrow the focus. You separate the issue from the intensity surrounding it.

A calm voice in a loud room has disproportionate influence. Not because it is soft—but because it signals control. Emotional escalation is rarely solved by emotional force. It is solved by disciplined framing. When someone shouts, "This is unacceptable!" the seasoned negotiator does not counter-shout. They respond with containment: "Let's define what specifically is unacceptable."

Volume meets clarity and intensity meets structure. The line is not drawn against the person. It is drawn against chaos.

The Pitfall

Mistaking calm for weakness—or aggression for power.

When voices rise, most people fall into one of two traps.

The first is escalation. They match tone with tone, believing authority requires volume. This produces a spiral. Each side feels justified. Each side feels disrespected. Substance disappears, and the negotiation becomes a contest of dominance.

The second trap is retreat. They lower their voice not from discipline but from fear. They concede prematurely, change positions abruptly, or allow process violations simply to quiet the room.

Both reactions surrender leverage. Escalation sacrifices composure. Retreat sacrifices boundaries. The deeper mistake is believing that emotional intensity equals power. It does not. It signals urgency, insecurity, or loss of perceived control. Those who cannot regulate their volume are often signaling that they cannot regulate the situation.

Another common error is trying to "win" the emotional moment. Correcting tone. Calling out behavior. Saying, "Calm down." This almost always backfires. People do not calm down when told to. They calm down when they feel heard and when structure is restored.

The moment you make the rising voice the issue, you shift from negotiation to behavioral policing. Hold your line through behavior - not lectures.

The Pointer

Control pace, protect process, anchor to standards.

There are three disciplined moves that allow you to hold the line when voices rise.

1. Lower Your Voice, Not Your Standard. A quiet, measured tone forces others to lean in rather than push back. It signals that you are not destabilized. But lowering your voice does not mean lowering your expectations.

"I'm prepared to work through this but I'm not prepared to rush this." The tone stays calm. The boundary stays firm.

2. Re-anchor to Process. Escalation often coincides with attempts to bypass process, introducing new demands, compressing timelines, or forcing immediate concessions. When that happens, return to structure. Process is neutral. It provides safety. It prevents the loudest voice from controlling the outcome.
   - "We agreed we would address scope before price."
   - "Let's resolve this issue before moving to the next."
   - "We can continue this conversation when we're

both ready to focus on solutions."

3. Slow the Tempo. Speed amplifies emotion. Slowing the conversation reduces heat.
    - Ask clarifying questions.
    - Take notes visibly.
    - Then summarize what you heard. When you say, "Let me make sure I understand your concern," you are not yielding. You are regulating the pace. You are signaling that nothing moves forward until clarity is achieved. Slowing down is not delay. It is discipline.

Holding the line when voices rise is not about silencing others. It is about refusing to let emotional intensity dictate decision quality. In high-stakes negotiations—especially where identity, status, or significant resources are involved—voices will rise. That is not failure. It is human. The test is not whether escalation happens. The test is whether you abandon structure when it does.

A steady negotiator becomes the stabilizing force in the room. Others may not immediately mirror your calm, but they will orient to it. Emotional volatility burns energy quickly. Composure endures.

INSIGHT 19 - THE POWER OF SILENCE

Silence makes most negotiators uncomfortable.

We are conditioned to fill space. In meetings, on job sites, across conference tables - whoever talks feels productive, engaged, and in control. Silence feels like a void. It feels like weakness. It feels like you're losing momentum.

Seasoned negotiators know better. They know silence is not empty. It is pressure. It is information. It is discipline.

The Principle

Silence creates leverage and reveals truth.

Silence is not the absence of communication. It is a form of communication.

When you stop talking, after making an offer, after asking a question, after hearing an accusation, you shift the psychological burden to the other side. Most people feel compelled to fill silence. In that filling, they reveal priorities, insecurities, constraints, and sometimes concessions. Silence does three powerful things.

First, it slows the tempo. Negotiations often escalate because speed replaces thought. Silence forces reflection. It lowers emotional temperature and allows rational processing to catch up with reactive impulses.

Second, it transfers pressure. If you make an offer and immediately start justifying it, you relieve the other side of the work of responding. If you make the offer and stop talking, the responsibility to speak falls on them.

Third, it exposes what matters. Ask a direct question, "What specifically is unacceptable about this proposal?" and then wait. The initial answer may be surface-level. But if you stay silent, they often go deeper. People clarify when given space. They soften when they hear their own rigidity. They reconsider when no one interrupts their thought.

Silence is also a test of confidence. When you can sit comfortably after stating your position, you signal certainty. You signal preparation. You signal that your proposal can withstand scrutiny.

The power of silence lies in restraint. Not dramatic silence. Not theatrical silence. Disciplined silence.

The Pitfall

Talking to relieve your own discomfort.

The greatest threat to the power of silence is your own anxiety.

After making a proposal, you feel the quiet stretch. Two seconds. Three seconds. It feels much longer. Your mind interprets the silence as rejection, confusion, or disapproval. To rescue yourself, you begin explaining:

"What I mean is,"

- "And of course we're flexible on...," or
- "We could possibly adjust...,"

In trying to reduce tension, you negotiate against yourself.

Another common mistake is using silence as a weapon. Some negotiators attempt to intimidate with prolonged, cold stares or exaggerated pauses. This shifts silence from disciplined presence to manipulation. Instead of encouraging thought, it triggers defensiveness.

There is also the danger of misreading silence. Silence does not always mean agreement. It does not always mean pressure is working. Sometimes silence means confusion. Sometimes it means disengagement. Sometimes it means the other party is processing internally or waiting strategically.

If you assume silence equals consent, you may walk away with false confidence. If you assume silence equals hostility, you may escalate unnecessarily.

The pitfall is not silence itself. The pitfall is reacting to silence - yours or theirs - without awareness.

The Pointer

Ask, state, stop.

The practical discipline of silence can be captured in three words: Ask, State, Stop. When you ask a question, stop talking. Let the answer form fully. If the response is incomplete, resist the urge to rescue it. Count slowly in your head if you must. Five seconds of silence can feel like an eternity, but it often produces clarity.

When you state a position, stop talking. No immediate defense. No justification unless requested. Let the proposal land. If it is reasonable and prepared, it does not need instant cushioning. When you hear something provocative, an accusation, a demand, a raised voice, pause before responding. A brief silence communicates composure. It signals that you are choosing your response rather than reacting.

You can also use calibrated silence. If someone finishes speaking and the room goes quiet, wait a beat longer than feels comfortable. Often, they will continue, refining or moderating their position. Silence is particularly powerful after someone makes an extreme statement. Instead of countering immediately, pause. Let the weight of their own words settle in the room. Frequently, they will soften it themselves. But silence must be paired with presence. Maintain eye contact. Nod subtly to show engagement. Silence should communicate attention, not withdrawal.

Used well, silence reduces unnecessary conflict. It prevents overexposure of your position. It encourages the other side to clarify and sometimes to concede. It allows thinking to replace reflex. In negotiation, words move pieces. Silence moves people.

Most negotiators try to win with better arguments. The seasoned negotiator understands that restraint is often more persuasive than rhetoric. Silence is not weakness. It is control. And in high-stakes conversations, control of yourself is the only control you truly have.

INSIGHT 20 – WHEN TO WALK AND WHEN NOT TO

Every negotiator eventually faces the moment of decision: stay at the table or stand up and leave. Walking away can be a power move. It can also be a catastrophic misread.

The seasoned negotiator knows that leaving is not an emotional reaction. It is a strategic act. And like all strategy, it must be grounded in clarity, not frustration.

When is walking strength, when it is sabotage, and how to know the difference.

The Principle

Walk only from strength, never from heat

Walking away is effective only when three conditions are present:

1. You have a real alternative. Not a hypothetical one. Not a pride-based fantasy. A real, viable path forward if this deal dies.
2. You are clear on your threshold. You know the numbers, terms, or conditions that make the agreement acceptable—or unacceptable.
3. Your departure communicates information. It signals seriousness, limits, and discipline—not volatility.

Walking away is not about punishment. It is about alignment.

In construction negotiations, for example, a subcontractor may threaten to walk from a project over payment terms. If that subcontractor has other committed work lined up, understands their cash flow exposure, and knows their margin floor, walking may be rational. But if they are walking because they "feel disrespected," or because the other party pushed hard, they are reacting—not deciding. The difference matters.

Walking from heat feels powerful in the moment. Walking from strength reshapes the negotiation.

When you leave strategically, you change the leverage dynamic. You force the other side to confront loss. You demonstrate that your participation is voluntary - not desperate.

But here is the paradox: the ability to walk often gives you the confidence to stay. When you truly know you can leave, you negotiate differently. You become calmer. Less reactive. More disciplined. You stop chasing agreement and start evaluating it. That posture alone changes outcomes.

The Pitfall

Mistaking ego protection for strategic exit.

The most common mistake negotiators make is walking to protect pride.

Someone anchors aggressively, someone questions your competence, someone issues a deadline or subtle threat and suddenly the internal voice says, I don't need this. So, you leave. But what actually happened? You reacted to identity threat, not deal reality. Walking to avoid discomfort feels principled. It often is not. It is simply ego seeking relief.

Another version of this pitfall is performative walking - storming out to pressure the other side, assuming they will chase you. Sometimes they do. Sometimes they let you go. If your exit depends on the other side rescuing the deal, you were never negotiating from strength.

There is also the opposite error: refusing to walk when you should.

Negotiators sometimes stay too long because they:

- fear appearing difficult, or
- because sunk costs whisper, we've come this far or
- because optimism overrides math.

In job-site disputes, this shows up when a contractor continues absorbing change-order risk long after the numbers no longer make sense, hoping relationship goodwill will eventually compensate for mounting exposure. It rarely does. Staying when your threshold has been breached erodes credibility - both externally and internally. If you signal limits but never enforce them, your future warnings lose weight.

The table learns that your "line" is flexible. And so do you.

The Pointer

Separate the signal from the emotion.

Before you walk, or decide not to, pause and ask three disciplined questions:

1. Has my objective threshold truly been crossed? Not "Am I irritated?" Not "Do I feel slighted?" But: Does this deal fail my defined criteria? If you cannot articulate the threshold clearly, you are not ready to walk.
2. What message will my departure send? Will it communicate clarity and discipline or volatility and unpredictability? Walking is a form of communication. Make sure it says what you intend.
3. What happens next, realistically? Do you have an executable alternative? Will walking advance your interests, or merely reset the conflict?

Sometimes the most powerful move is not leaving the negotiation entirely - but reframing it. Instead of "We're done," it might sound like: "At these terms, we can't move forward. If conditions change, we're open to revisiting." This preserves dignity. It preserves optionality. It keeps the door ajar without surrendering position. And sometimes the strongest move is staying, calmly.

When the other side tests you with pressure, your steadiness can be more disruptive than departure. Refusing to escalate when escalation is invited often exposes manufactured urgency or hollow threats. Walking is not strength. Discipline is strength.

There are moments when walking is necessary:

- When ethics are compromised.
- When financial exposure exceeds tolerance.
- When trust is irreparably broken.
- When your alternative is genuinely better.

There are moments when staying is wiser:

- When tension is temporary.
- When terms are still fluid.
- When emotion, not substance is driving conflict.
- When silence and patience will yield more information.

The seasoned negotiator does not ask, "Should I win this standoff?" They ask, "What move best advances my long-term position?" Sometimes that move is the door. Sometimes it is the chair. Knowing the difference is not about courage. It is about clarity.

CHAPTER THREE

POWER, RIGHTS, AND INTERESTS

"Seasoned negotiators know something others learn the hard way: Not everyone who decides is present and not everyone who is present decides."

Insight 21. Understanding Structural Power

Insight 22. Informational Power

Insight 23. Relational Power

Insight 24. Authority vs. Influence Insight 25. The Hidden Veto

Insight 26. BATNA in the Real World

Insight 27. The Cost of Overplaying Leverage

Insight 28. Legitimacy and Standards

Insight 29. Power That Doesn't Look Like Power

INSIGHT 21 - UNDERSTANDING STRUCTURAL POWER

Most negotiators are trained to think about personality, persuasion, and tactics. Few are trained to see the architecture of the room itself. Yet, long before anyone raises a voice or makes a demand, the structure has already tilted the table.

Structural power is not loud. It does not argue. It does not threaten. It simply shapes what is possible. If you do not see it, you will misread everything else.

The Principle

Power is embedded in the structure, not just the people.

Structural power lives in systems - contracts, roles, deadlines, information flow, precedent, access to capital, regulatory authority, and decision-making processes. It exists independent of temperament. A calm executive can hold enormous power. A charismatic project manager may have very little.

On a construction project, structural power often sits in three places:

- Control of the schedule.
- Control of payment.
- Control of scope interpretation.

Consider a subcontractor negotiating a change order. The general contractor may appear cooperative, even friendly. But if the subcontractor is cash-flow constrained and payment approval sits entirely within the GC's process, the structure already favors one side. Add a looming milestone date tied to liquidated damages, and urgency becomes another lever embedded in the system. No one has to threaten. The schedule does that.

Structural power also hides in decision pathways. Who must approve what? Who can delay without consequence? Who absorbs risk if nothing changes? If one party can afford to wait and the other cannot, patience itself becomes power. The seasoned negotiator does not begin with personalities. They begin with structure.

They ask:

- Who controls timing?
- Who controls information?
- Who controls consequences?
- Who can walk away?

- Who pays if these stall?

The answers to those questions explain behavior more accurately than tone ever will.

The Pitfall

Mistaking positional strength for personal strength.

The common mistake is personalizing structural power. When one side pushes hard, delays approvals, or refuses concessions, the instinct is to label them as aggressive, unreasonable, or arrogant. In reality, they may simply be operating from a structurally advantaged position.

This misreading leads to two dangerous reactions.

First, escalation. If you assume the other party is being difficult by choice, you respond with counter-pressure. But pressure applied against structural advantage rarely works. It often hardens resistance.

Second, resentment. You feel disrespected. You feel unheard. But what you are experiencing may not be disrespect. It may be asymmetry.

On the job site, this plays out when a subcontractor believes the project manager is "playing games" with change order approvals. The PM, however, may be bound by an owner approval process two levels up. The subcontractor sees obstruction. The PM sees constraint. Both react emotionally to what is actually structural.

Another version occurs when senior leadership enters a negotiation late and reverses field-level agreements. The team feels betrayed. But the structural hierarchy always reserved final authority at the top. The mistake was confusing delegated discussion with delegated power.

When negotiators ignore structure, they argue about fairness while the system quietly dictates outcomes and systems are not persuaded by emotion.

The Pointer

Map the structure before you make a move.

Before you push, pause. Draw the map - literally, if necessary.

List the stakeholders. Identify formal authority. Trace decision approval chains. Clarify contractual rights. Identify timing pressures. Examine who carries financial exposure. Note who has alternatives outside this deal.

When you do this, three strategic options become clearer:

1. Work within the structure. If the other side has legitimate authority over payment, adjust your proposal to align with their process rather than fighting it.
2. Shift the structure. If the schedule is being used as leverage, can sequencing be adjusted? Can milestones be renegotiated? Can partial approvals reduce bottlenecks?
3. Balance the structure. If you lack financial leverage, can you increase informational leverage? If you lack authority, can you engage someone who has it?

Seasoned negotiators understand that you rarely defeat structural power head-on. You either reposition yourself within it or alter the conditions that give it strength. They also manage their own structural blind spots.

Ask yourself:

- Am I assuming authority I don't actually have?
- Am I negotiating with someone who cannot decide?
- Am I relying on urgency that the other side does not feel?
- Am I mistaking temporary pressure for permanent power?

Structural power shifts over time. Cash flow changes, deadlines pass, leadership rotates, market conditions tighten or loosen. What was once dominant can weaken quickly. But only if you notice.

Structural power is the invisible framework beneath every negotiation. It determines who waits comfortably and who sweats. Who absorbs risk and who transfers it. Who must answer to others and who answers to no one in the room. Understanding structural power does not make you cynical. It makes you precise. When you see the structure clearly, you stop arguing about personality. You stop reacting to tone. You stop taking resistance personally. Instead, you negotiate with the system itself. And that is where real leverage lives.

INSIGHT 22 – INFORMATIONAL POWER

There is a form of power in negotiation that does not shout, threaten, or demand. It does not sit at the head of the table and it rarely announces itself.

Informational power is the quiet advantage held by the party who understands more about the facts, the pressures, the timelines, the personalities, and the alternatives in play. It is not positional authority. It is not financial leverage. It is not legal strength. It is clarity, and clarity changes everything.

The Principle

Information is leverage—but only when it is accurate, relevant, and strategically used.

Every negotiation is shaped by three things: (1) what is known, (2) what is assumed, and (3) what is hidden. The seasoned negotiator understands that information falls into categories:

- Objective facts (budgets, deadlines, specifications, market data).
- Subjective drivers (fear, reputation, internal politics, career risk).
- Constraints (authority limits, approval chains, cash flow realities).
- Alternatives (what each side can realistically do if no deal is reached).

Most people gather information casually. The professional gathers it deliberately.

On a construction project, informational power might mean knowing that the owner's financing closes in 45 days. Or that the general contractor has three other trades behind schedule. Or that a subcontractor's backlog is thin going into winter. The information itself is neutral. But its implications are not.

If you know the other side's deadline is hard and yours is flexible, you negotiate differently. If you know a decision-maker must protect their internal reputation, you structure proposals that allow them to save face. Informational power reduces guesswork. It narrows uncertainty. It clarifies what actually matters. But information alone is not power. It becomes power when you understand how it shifts risk, urgency, and choice.

The Pitfall

Confusing volume of information with strategic advantage.

Many negotiators believe that more data equals more strength. They walk into meetings armed with binders, spreadsheets, emails, and historical precedent. They try to overwhelm. But information that is unfiltered, poorly timed, or irrelevant becomes noise. Worse, some negotiators misuse information as a weapon, springing surprises, withholding critical facts until the last minute, or attempting to embarrass the other side publicly.

Short-term advantage? Maybe. Long-term trust? Destroyed.

Another common mistake is overconfidence. A negotiator learns one critical fact - perhaps that the other party is under pressure - and assumes that single insight gives them total leverage. They push too hard. What they fail to consider is that information changes. Pressures shift. Alternatives emerge.

Informational power decays if it is not continuously updated. There is also a dangerous illusion in believing you understand the other side's constraints when you are merely projecting your own. Assumption masquerading as information is one of the fastest ways to miscalculate.

Finally, some negotiators hoard information instead of using it. They collect insights but never translate them into structured moves, questions, proposals, timing strategies, or concessions.

Information that sits unused in your notebook is not power. It is trivia.

The Pointer

Ask better questions than anyone else in the room and listen for what is not being said.

The strongest negotiators are not talkers first. They are investigators. They understand that informational power is rarely handed over voluntarily. It is revealed indirectly - through tone, hesitation, emphasis, and deflection.

When someone says, "That won't work," the seasoned negotiator asks, "Help me understand what makes it difficult." When someone insists on urgency, they explore: "What happens if this isn't resolved by then?" When someone claims they lack authority, they inquire: "Who needs to be comfortable with this?"

These questions are not interrogations. They are doorways. The goal is not to corner the other side. It is to map the terrain. In construction negotiations, informational power often comes from understanding sequencing. Which trade is truly critical path? Where are inspections scheduled? What material lead times are non-negotiable? Knowing the technical structure of the project often matters more than knowing the personalities involved.

At the same time, emotional data is just as powerful. Who feels exposed? Who feels blamed? Who cannot afford to "lose" publicly? Listen for pressure. Pressure reveals priority.

There is also a strategic discipline in deciding what information to share. Transparency builds credibility, but selective disclosure can create movement. Offering the right information at the right time can unlock stalled conversations. For example, revealing that you have flexibility in schedule, but not in price, redirects the conversation toward creative sequencing solutions instead of discount demands. Information, properly timed, reshapes the conversation. And perhaps most important: verify. Before acting on a key insight, test it gently. “It sounds like timing is more important than cost here, is that fair?” Confirmation prevents miscalculation.

Informational power is not about manipulation. It is about understanding reality more clearly than the other side expects you to. When you understand reality, you stop reacting emotionally. You stop posturing. You stop guessing and you begin choosing.

The loudest negotiator in the room often feels powerful but the best-informed negotiator actually is. In the end, informational power is not about controlling the other side. It is about controlling your own decisions because you see the board more clearly.

INSIGHT 23 - RELATIONAL POWER

Power in negotiation is often misunderstood. We tend to think of it as leverage, authority, money, contractual rights, or the ability to walk away. And yes, those matter, but in complex environments, especially in construction, executive leadership, labor relations, or

long-term partnerships, there is a quieter form of influence that outperforms brute leverage over time.

That force is relational power. Relational power is the ability to influence outcomes because of trust, credibility, reputation, and the quality of connection you have built. It is not imposed. It is earned. And once established, it becomes one of the most durable forms of negotiation advantage available.

The Principle

Relational power is built long before you need it and spent in moments of strain.

Most negotiations do not begin at the conference table. They begin in hallway conversations, job-site walkthroughs, shared problem-solving sessions, and the thousands of small interactions where people decide whether you are credible, fair, and steady under pressure.

Relational power grows from consistency:

- You do what you say you will do.
- You deliver difficult messages without humiliation.
- You protect the other side's dignity even when you disagree.
- You solve problems without keeping score.

Over time, people begin to grant you something rare: the benefit of the doubt. When conflict inevitably arrives, as it always does, the negotiator with relational capital does not start at zero. They start with credibility. Their words are not filtered through suspicion. Their proposals are not assumed to hide traps. Their pauses are not interpreted as manipulation.

Relational power lowers friction.

In a job-site dispute over schedule compression, for example, a superintendent with strong relational capital can say, "We need help here," and the trade partner hears collaboration—not accusation. A project manager with relational power can push back on change order pricing without triggering defensive escalation. A labor leader with relational standing can calm a heated meeting with a single sentence. Relational power does not eliminate conflict. It makes conflict manageable. Relational power increases precisely because you do not exploit it recklessly. When people see that you could pressure them, but choose instead to reason with them, they trust you more.

Power used sparingly becomes power amplified.

The Pitfall

Mistaking friendliness for relational strength.

Many professionals confuse being liked with having relational power. They avoid hard conversations in the name of preserving goodwill. They soften necessary boundaries. They delay accountability and they tolerate underperformance because they fear relational damage. This is not relational power. It is relational avoidance. True relational strength is not built on comfort. It is built on credibility. And credibility requires the willingness to confront issues directly and respectfully.

Another common mistake is transactional scorekeeping. "We gave you this last time." "You owe us." "Remember when we helped you?" The moment you weaponize past cooperation, you convert relational power into transactional leverage. And leverage, once exposed, weakens trust.

There is also a darker pitfall: assuming relational capital is permanent. It is not.

Relational power decays when:

- You surprise people with hidden agendas.
- You escalate without warning.
- You bypass established communication channels.
- You fail to repair small ruptures quickly.

Trust erodes quietly. Often you don't realize it is gone until you attempt to rely on it.

Finally, some negotiators underestimate relational power entirely. They rely exclusively on contractual rights or positional authority. They win arguments but lose influence. They secure concessions but damage long-term cooperation.

In industries built on repeat interaction, like construction, executive leadership, or labor-management negotiations, this is a costly error. You may win the issue and lose the relationship. And in recurring negotiations, that is rarely a victory.

The Pointer

Invest in the relationship when stakes are low so you can draw on it when stakes are high.

Relational power is accumulated intentionally. It does not happen by accident.

Three practical moves build it:

1. Make deposits when you do not need anything. Check in, offer assistance, share useful information, and acknowledge good performance. These gestures are not manipulation; they're maintenance.
2. Address tension early. Do not allow small resentments to harden. A five-minute clarifying conversation today prevents a five-hour confrontation next month.
3. Separate the person from the problem consistently. You can press hard on an issue while protecting dignity. "This number doesn't work for us" is different from "You're being unreasonable." Over time, people learn that disagreement with you does not equal disrespect.

And when the moment comes to assert leverage, and sometimes it does, you do so transparently. You explain the constraint, you signal the boundary, and you allow the other side to save face. Relational power allows firmness without hostility. The seasoned negotiator understands something fundamental: in most professional ecosystems, today's adversary may be tomorrow's partner. Reputation travels faster than email. And memory lasts longer than contracts.

Relational power is quiet. It does not boast. It does not threaten. It does not announce itself. But when pressure rises and conversations tighten, it is often the invisible force that determines whether negotiation becomes a breakdown or a breakthrough.

Build it early. Guard it carefully. Spend it wisely.

INSIGHT 24 - AUTHORITY VS. INFLUENCE

In high-stakes environments like construction, corporate leadership, or public service, people often confuse authority with influence. They assume the title carries the weight. They assume the organizational chart settles the matter. They assume that because they can decide, others will follow. But authority and influence are not the same currency.

Authority is granted. Influence is earned. Authority compels compliance. Influence invites commitment. Understanding the difference is not philosophical. It is practical. And it determines whether your agreements hold when you're not in the room.

The Principle

Authority gives you the right to decide. Influence gives you the ability to be followed.

Authority is positional power. It comes from a title, a contract, or a legal right. A project executive can direct a change order. A superintendent can shut down unsafe work. A labor leader can call a meeting, but this authority creates boundaries and sets decisions in motion.

Influence determines how those decisions land. You can order compliance. You cannot order trust. You can demand action but you cannot demand buy-in.

Authority moves paper. Influence moves people. The seasoned negotiator understands that authority is often necessary, but rarely sufficient. The most effective leaders know when to use their authority and when to rely on influence. They recognize that overuse of authority weakens influence over time.

When someone relies solely on positional power, the conversation narrows. People shift into defensive postures. They look for leverage, protection, or an exit. But when someone leads with influence, credibility, consistency, respect, and clarity, others voluntarily align.

Influence is built through three disciplines:

1. Competence - People trust those who understand the work.
2. Consistency - People follow those who act predictably under pressure.
3. Respect - People respond to those who preserve dignity.

Authority may get you immediate compliance. Influence builds durable alignment. And in complex negotiations, durability matters more than immediacy.

The Pitfall

Mistaking silence for agreement.

One of the most dangerous illusions in leadership is confusing compliance with commitment. You issue direction. The room goes quiet. Heads nod. No one pushes back.

You assume alignment, but silence is not agreement. Silence can mean hesitation, resentment, calculation or quiet resistance. When authority is heavy-handed, people comply publicly and resist privately. Deadlines slip. Enthusiasm evaporates. "Misunderstandings" multiply. You begin to hear, "That's what they told us to do," instead of, "Here's how we're making it work."

This is especially true in environments where hierarchy is strong. The more rigid the structure, the more likely people are to withhold concerns. Authority suppresses friction in the moment, but unresolved friction surfaces later as delay, cost, or conflict.

Another pitfall is the ego trap. Authority can inflate identity. The title becomes part of the self. Disagreement feels like disrespect. Questions feel like insubordination. So, authority is used to restore order - quickly and decisively. But each time authority substitutes for persuasion, influence erodes. Over time, leaders who lean too heavily on authority create compliance cultures, not performance cultures. People wait to be told. Initiative declines. Risk-taking disappears. Problems travel upward instead of being solved at the level where they occur.

And when real crisis hits, authority alone cannot mobilize discretionary effort but influence can.

The Pointer

Use authority sparingly. Invest in influence daily.

Seasoned negotiators treat authority like a fire extinguisher.

Necessary, visible, but rarely used.

They don't hide it nor do they lead with it. When entering a negotiation, they ask themselves: "Do I need to assert authority here, or can I shape alignment?"

Instead of saying, "This is the direction," they say, "Here's the constraint we're operating under. Let's figure out the best way through it." Instead of, "Because I said so," they offer reasoning.

Instead of closing a debate prematurely, they invite perspective before deciding. Influence grows when people feel heard - even if the final decision is not theirs. This does not mean abandoning authority. There are moments when safety, legality, or strategic clarity demand decisive direction. In those moments, strong authority prevents chaos. But after the directive, influence rebuilds alignment.

The seasoned negotiator also understands timing. Influence is slow capital. It compounds over time through small behaviors:

- Following through on commitments.
- Owning mistakes without defensiveness.
- Protecting others' dignity during disagreement.
- Separating disagreement from disrespect.
- Communicating intent before impact hardens perception.

Influence is relational equity. The more influence you build, the less you need to use authority.

People who trust your judgment will follow direction with

less resistance. People who believe you respect them will accept difficult decisions with greater resilience. People who feel included will defend agreements in your absence.

Authority establishes order. Influence sustains it. In negotiation, both matter. But they operate differently. Authority can secure the decision. Influence secures the future.

If you rely only on what your title gives you, your power shrinks when your position changes. But if you invest in influence, credibility, fairness, clarity, and restraint, your impact travels with you. When authority and influence align, when people follow not because they must, but because they believe, that is when negotiation moves beyond compliance into commitment.

That is when agreements hold.

INSIGHT 25 - THE HIDDEN VETO

Every negotiation has visible players, the ones at the table, the ones on the email chain or the ones back at the respective offices. Seasoned negotiators know something others learn the hard way: Not everyone who decides is present and not everyone who is present decides.

That unseen influence is what I call The Hidden Veto. It is the silent "no" that can kill an agreement long after everyone in the room said "yes."

The Principle

Decisions are made in systems, not meetings.

Most people negotiate as if agreement in the room equals resolution in reality. It does not. Organizations are systems of authority, politics, incentives, pride, history, and fear. The superintendent may nod. The project manager may agree. The union steward may soften. The supplier may concede. But somewhere else sits someone who was not consulted - and who retains the power to undo everything.

The hidden veto often belongs to:

- An executive protecting margin.
- A legal department guarding precedent.
- A spouse worried about risk.
- A disgruntled union member.
- A senior partner preserving status.
- A silent investor concerned about optics.
- A foreman whose crew will refuse to cooperate.

The key insight is simple: authority is rarely linear. Influence moves sideways, backward, and informally. Agreements collapse not because terms were flawed, but because legitimacy was incomplete.

In complex environments, construction, corporate negotiations, public contracts, or labor environments - you are not negotiating with a person. You are negotiating with a web. The seasoned negotiator assumes that every "yes" is provisional until the system has absorbed it.

They ask:

- Who else must live with this?
- Who feels threatened by this?
- Who loses status if this succeeds?
- Who benefits if this fails?

If you do not identify the hidden veto early, it will identify you later.

The Pitfall

Mistaking access for authority.

The most common mistake is assuming that the person across from you has the power they appear to hold. Access feels like authority.

You are in the room. You are discussing numbers. Draft language is being edited. There is apparent movement. The tone is constructive so you relax. Then three days later you hear: "Leadership isn't comfortable with this." "Legal won't approve it." "The board has concerns," or "My partner doesn't see it that way."

What happened? You negotiated with a messenger. Or worse, you negotiated with someone who thought they had authority but didn't.

Another version of the pitfall is ego-driven blindness. People avoid asking about other decision-makers because they do not want to appear weak. They assume that pressing for confirmation will undermine momentum. So, they skip the uncomfortable question: "Who else needs to sign off on this?" And the deal dies quietly in a hallway you never walked down.

On a job-site, this might look like agreeing on a change order with a project manager, only to have accounting reject it because it violates internal cost controls. Or reaching a scheduling compromise with a superintendent, only to have ownership refuse because it impacts financing triggers. The meeting was real, the agreement was real, the authority was not.

The hidden veto thrives in unasked questions.

The Pointer

Surface the system before you solve the substance.

Seasoned negotiators normalize the authority conversation early. They do not interrogate. They clarify.

They say things like:

- "Help me understand how decisions get finalized on your side."
- "Who else will weigh in on this before it's done?"
- "If we reach agreement here, what happens next internally?"
- "Is there anyone not in this room who could see this differently?"

Notice the tone. Not accusatory - not skeptical - simply procedural.

This does three things:

1. It protects momentum. You discover obstacles before you build commitments around them.
2. It preserves face. You allow the other party to admit limits without embarrassment.
3. It expands coalition. You may learn that someone influential needs to be brought in early, not after resistance hardens.

Another advanced move is to ask your counterpart what objections they expect internally. "What pushback do you anticipate?" This question transforms them from gatekeeper to an ally. You are now solving the hidden veto together. If they say, "Finance will never go for that," you now have actionable data. You can adjust framing, timing, structure, or risk allocation before the veto becomes final.

And sometimes the hidden veto is emotional rather than structural. A senior leader may feel bypassed. A foreman may feel disrespected. A partner may feel loss of control. These unspoken reactions can override logic. Surfacing them requires humility and curiosity, not force. The ultimate discipline is this: never confuse agreement with approval. Until you understand how your counterpart's system digests decisions, the negotiation is incomplete.

The Hidden Veto is not sabotage, it is structure. It is not betrayal, it is reality. Negotiation is rarely about convincing the person in front of you. It is about ensuring that the agreement can survive the people behind them. If you ignore the unseen, you will repeatedly win conversations and lose outcomes. But if you respect the system, map it, surface it, and incorporate it, your agreements will not just sound good in the room. They will hold when the room is empty.

INSIGHT 26 - BATNA IN THE REAL WORLD

BATNA - Best Alternative to a Negotiated Agreement - is one of the most quoted concepts in negotiation. It comes from the work of Roger Fisher and William Ury in their landmark book Getting to Yes.

In theory, BATNA is simple: if the deal on the table is worse than your alternative, you walk. If it's better, you sign. In the real world, it is rarely that clean.

On job-sites, in executive suites, and across bargaining tables, BATNA is not a static calculation. It is emotional, political, imperfectly informed, and often misunderstood. The disciplined negotiator respects BATNA - but does not worship it.

The Principle

Your power is defined by your realistic alternative, not your preferred outcome.

BATNA is about leverage. Not bluster. Not threat. Not hope. Your power in a negotiation is determined by what you can credibly do if this agreement fails.

If a contractor can replace a subcontractor within two weeks at a reasonable cost, that is leverage. If the subcontractor can walk to three other active projects tomorrow, that is leverage. If either party believes they have options but cannot execute them, that is fantasy.

In the real world, BATNA has three dimensions:

1. Quality - Is the alternative truly better? Or just less painful?
2. Credibility - Can you actually execute it?
3. Cost - Financial, relational, reputational, and time cost.

Most negotiators calculate only price. Seasoned negotiators calculate impact. For example, terminating a subcontractor mid-project may look like a strong BATNA on paper. But what about:

- Delay exposure?
- Replacement risk?
- Litigation?
- Damage to labor relationships?
- Signal to other trades?

The real BATNA is not the legal right to terminate. It is the total consequence of doing so. The disciplined negotiator does not ask, “Can we?” They ask, “What really happens if we do?” That question changes everything.

The Pitfall

Inflating your BATNA - or ignoring theirs.

There are two common errors with BATNA.

First, overestimating your own. Ego, optimism, and selective information inflate alternatives. A project manager may believe, "We'll just replace them," without accounting for procurement time, learning curves, and disruption. A union rep may think, "We can strike," without fully calculating member tolerance for lost wages.

An inflated BATNA produces rigid positions and premature escalation. When someone says, "We don't need this deal," the seasoned negotiator silently asks: Are you sure?

The second mistake is ignoring the other side's BATNA. Many negotiators focus exclusively on strengthening their alternatives while failing to understand the other party. That blindness leads to misreads. If the other side has no viable alternative, they may become desperate and unpredictable. If their BATNA is strong, they may appear stubborn when they are simply rational.

You cannot negotiate effectively against a BATNA you have not mapped. And here is the uncomfortable truth: sometimes their BATNA is better than yours. In those moments, power shifts. The goal is no longer domination. It becomes damage control, value creation, or a graceful exit. Ignoring reality does not improve leverage. It merely delays recognition of it.

The Pointer

Strengthen yours quietly, test theirs gently.

Seasoned negotiators treat BATNA as strategy, not theater.

First, strengthen your alternative without announcing it. Secure backup vendors, build internal consensus, line up financing, prepare contingency plans, but resist the temptation to threaten. Announced BATNAs often harden positions. Quiet ones preserve flexibility.

Second, test the other side's BATNA without direct confrontation.

Instead of saying, "You can't replace us," ask:

- "How would that transition work?"
- "What timeline would that require?"
- "Who would handle continuity?"

Calibrated questions reveal feasibility gaps without accusation.

Third, evaluate timing. A weak BATNA today may strengthen tomorrow. A strong one may erode. Real-world negotiation is dynamic. Market shifts, labor supply, regulatory changes - these factors alter leverage constantly. The disciplined negotiator revisits BATNA calculations throughout the process. They do not rely on assumptions formed at the outset.

Finally, remember this: BATNA is not just a walk-away plan. It is a confidence stabilizer. When you know your alternative, you are less reactive, less emotional and less desperate. That composure alone improves your performance. In textbooks, BATNA is a clean comparison. In the field, it is layered with:

- Pride

- Fear
- Politics
- Uncertainty
- Reputation

Sometimes walking away damages more than signing a flawed deal. Sometimes signing a flawed deal locks in years of compounded cost. The experienced negotiator does not treat BATNA as an escape hatch. They treat it as a lens.

BATNA in the real world is not about bravado. It is about clarity.

INSIGHT 27 – THE COST OF OVERPLAYING LEVERAGE

Leverage is intoxicating.

When you know the schedule cannot move without you, when funding is locked in and time is short, or when the other side has fewer options than you do, it is tempting to press hard. To extract concessions. To remind them, subtly or not, who holds the advantage.

In negotiation, leverage is real. But it is also perishable. And when it is overplayed, it does not simply weaken a relationship, it can collapse value, trigger retaliation, and damage reputations that took years to build.

The Principle

Leverage is a tool, not a weapon.

Leverage comes from asymmetry, of alternatives, information, timing, authority, or need. It may come from a stronger BATNA, market scarcity, political backing, or operational control. In construction, it might be control of a critical path activity. In labor relations, it may be public sentiment. In business, it may be access to capital. But leverage is most powerful when it is felt, not flaunted.

Seasoned negotiators understand that leverage works best when it shapes expectations quietly. They do not announce it; they design around it. They do not humiliate the other side; they give them a path to agreement that preserves dignity. That's because today's leverage often becomes tomorrow's vulnerability.

A subcontractor squeezed to the breaking point may comply, but productivity drops. A union cornered in public may settle, but they will remember. A vendor forced into thin margins may prioritize other clients when shortages arise. Leverage can produce compliance. It rarely produces commitment. The principle is simple: use leverage to protect your interests, not to punish the other side.

Restraint signals confidence. It communicates that you are strong enough not to dominate. And that is a different kind of power.

The Pitfall

Winning the round and losing the relationship.

The most common mistake is confusing advantage with entitlement. When negotiators sense leverage, they often escalate demands. They widen the ask. They press for symbolic victories. They move from "what is fair" to "what can I get away with?"

Overplaying leverage typically shows up in three ways:

1. Public pressure. Forcing the other side to concede in front of stakeholders, media, or their own team.
2. Maximalist demands. Extracting every possible concession because the moment allows it.
3. Dismissive tone. Communicating, directly or indirectly, that the other side has no real choice.

The short-term result may look like a win. The long-term consequences are less visible, but more costly. The other side begins looking for ways to rebalance the equation. They search for alternatives. They delay future cooperation. They comply minimally and they remember.

In ongoing relationships, construction projects, labor partnerships, supply chains, joint ventures - the negotiation is never truly over. Overplayed leverage plant seeds of future resistance. And here is the deeper cost: reputation. In tight professional communities, word travels. Contractors talk. Vendors talk. Labor leaders talk. Executives compare notes. A pattern of squeezing others when the market shifts will eventually define you.

Markets cycle. Leverage rotates. And when the pendulum swings, and it always does, the memory of how you used your advantage becomes part of the next negotiation. Overplaying leverage does not just strain one deal. It erodes your long-term bargaining position.

The Pointer

Convert leverage into stability.

If you have leverage, use it strategically. Convert temporary advantage into durable structure. Instead of asking, "How much can I extract?" ask, "How can I lock in stability?"

Here are three practical moves:

1. Anchor firmly, concede thoughtfully. Start strong, but signal flexibility. Let the other side experience your advantage without being crushed by it. Make concessions deliberately and tie them to reciprocal commitments.
2. Protect Face. Never force unnecessary humiliation. Give the other side a narrative they can take back to their stakeholders. Agreements that preserve dignity last longer.
3. Trade Power for Performance. If you control timing or access, use that leverage to secure performance guarantees, communication standards, risk-sharing mechanisms, or future collaboration frameworks, not just price reductions.

In other words, transform leverage into systems. A contractor who could demand punitive terms instead negotiates clarity around scope changes. A union with strike power negotiates safety commitments and communication channels. A supplier in short supply secures multi-year agreements instead of opportunistic markups.

This is how professionals think. They recognize that leverage is temporary, but relationships and reputations compound. Restraint is not weakness. It is strategic maturity. Leverage will always be part of negotiation. Power asymmetries are unavoidable. The question is not whether you have it, but how you use it. Overplaying leverage feels strong in the moment. It can produce visible, measurable gains. But it also narrows trust, reduces cooperation, and invites future resistance. The most seasoned negotiators understand something counterintuitive: the stronger their position, the more carefully they behave.

They press, but not to the breaking point. They claim value, but leave room for mutual sustainability. They assert strength, but avoid domination. In complex, ongoing environments, like construction, labor relations, and executive leadership, the real win is not extracting the last concession. It is building agreements that hold when circumstances change. Leverage wins rounds restraint wins careers.

INSIGHT 28 - LEGITIMACY AND STANDARDS

In every serious negotiation, someone eventually says, “That’s not fair.”

What they are really asking is not for charity. They’re asking for legitimacy.

The seasoned negotiator understands that power can move a conversation but legitimacy settles it. Standards that are external, recognized, and defensible turn opinion into credibility. They shift the discussion from what I want to what makes sense. And that shift changes everything.

The Principle

Anchor agreements in objective standards.

Legitimacy is built on standards that exist outside the personalities at the table - market rates, industry norms, historical practice, written policy, precedent, legal guidance and independent expert opinion. When you anchor your proposal to something both sides recognize as legitimate, you remove ego from the equation.

Instead of saying, “This is what I need,” you say, “This is consistent with how similar projects are structured.” Instead of, “Your price is too high,” you say, “Comparable contracts in this region are landing between X and Y.” Standards create gravity. They pull the conversation toward reason.

On a construction project, for example, a subcontractor demanding additional compensation for scope expansion may feel like a standoff. If the general contractor responds emotionally, “That’s excessive,” the conflict escalates. But if the discussion pivots to contract language, documented change orders, and historical unit pricing from similar jobs, the tone changes. The debate becomes analytical instead of personal.

Objective criteria don’t eliminate disagreement. They discipline it. They also protect relationships. When both parties can point to a standard, neither feels personally attacked. You are not conceding to the other side - you are aligning with a principle larger than both of you. And that is the power of legitimacy.

The Pitfall

Using standards as weapons instead of guides.

There is a subtle but dangerous mistake negotiators make with standards: they weaponize them. They cherry-pick favorable data. They cite "industry norms" without context. They lean on policy as if it were a shield against conversation. Instead of building legitimacy, they build resentment. When standards are used to corner someone rather than guide the discussion, trust erodes.

Consider a project manager who says, "The contract clearly states..." and then refuses to explore practical realities on the ground. Technically correct. Relationally tone-deaf. In a labor negotiation where one side insists, "the market rate is this," without acknowledging differences in geography, risk allocation, or scope complexity, the standard may be real, but incomplete. Standards are persuasive only when both sides believe they are being applied fairly.

Another common error is mistaking authority for legitimacy. Just because you can enforce a clause doesn't mean you should. Courts and contracts provide rights; negotiations require judgment. If you hide behind technicalities, you may win the point and lose the partnership.

Legitimacy must feel mutual. If only one party believes in the standard being used, it isn't a standard - it's leverage dressed up as fairness, and that rarely holds.

The Pointer

Invite the other side into the standard.

The most effective way to use legitimacy is collaborative, not declarative. Instead of announcing the standard, ask:

"What benchmarks do you think are fair for evaluating this?" or "how do similar projects handle this risk?" or "what would an independent expert say about this structure?" When the other side participates in selecting the criteria, they are far more likely to accept the outcome. This approach does three things:

1. It surfaces hidden assumptions.
2. It builds shared ownership of the framework.
3. It reduces defensive posture.

In high-stakes negotiations, particularly in construction where margins are tight and reputations matter, shared standards protect long-term relationships. They allow hard conversations without hardening positions.

It is also wise to prepare multiple legitimate anchors before entering the room. Prepare market data, policy references, comparable deals and risk analyses. If one standard is challenged, you have others ready, not as ammunition, but as options.

And when you are on the weaker side of a power imbalance, legitimacy becomes your equalizer. A small subcontractor negotiating with a large developer may lack leverage - but if the subcontractor can ground requests in documented precedent and industry norms, the playing field narrows. Standards give structure to fairness.

Finally, be willing to test your own proposal against the same criteria. Ask yourself: "If roles were reversed, would I accept this as reasonable?" If the answer is no, your standard may not be as objective as you think. Legitimacy begins with intellectual honesty.

In the end, negotiations rarely collapse because people lack arguments. They collapse because they lack shared principles. Power may start the conversation. Rights may define its boundaries. But legitimacy sustains agreement. When you root your proposals in standards that both sides can respect, and when you apply them with humility rather than force, you elevate the negotiation from a contest of wills to a process of reasoning. And reasoning, unlike pressure, tends to endure.

INSIGHT 29 – POWER THAT DOESN'T LOOK LIKE POWER

Power is often imagined as something obvious - the title on the door, signatures on contracts, the authority to say yes or no. But in real negotiations, the most decisive power rarely announces itself. It doesn't sit at the head of the table. It doesn't raise its voice. And it

doesn't always carry a formal title. The power that changes outcomes most often is subtle, relational, informational, or procedural. It hides in plain sight.

The Principle

Power is the ability to shape the field.

Power is not merely the authority to decide. It is the ability to shape the environment in which decisions are made. A superintendent who controls sequencing on a jobsite may not control the budget, but they control timing. A project engineer who manages documentation may not negotiate final terms, but they influence what is recorded, framed, and escalated. An administrative assistant who controls access to a senior executive does not vote on strategy, but they shape who gets heard and when.

These actors rarely look powerful. Yet they shape the field. In complex negotiations, outcomes are influenced by:

- Who frames the problem first.
- Who controls the information flow.
- Who defines what is "reasonable."
- Who sets the meeting agenda.
- Who summarizes the discussion at the end.

These are not ceremonial roles. They are leverage points. The seasoned negotiator understands that formal authority is only one type of power. Informational control, relational trust, procedural access, and reputational credibility are often stronger. They move decisions without appearing to force them. Subtle power works because it operates upstream. Instead of fighting over the final decision, it influences how the decision is constructed.

When you shape the field, you shape the outcome.

The Pitfall

Ignoring the quiet influencers.

The common mistake is focusing only on visible authority. Negotiators often obsess over "the decision-maker" and ignore everyone else. They assume that if they can persuade the person with the title, the deal is done. But decisions are rarely made in isolation. They are filtered, interpreted, and influenced long before they reach the formal signer.

The quiet influencer can be:

- The trusted advisor who the executive confides in.
- The field leader whose buy-in determines implementation.
- The union steward who signals whether an agreement will hold.
- The finance analyst who prepares the risk summary.
- The client representative who shapes perception internally.

None of these roles may have formal veto power. Yet each can delay, distort, or derail momentum. The pitfall deepens when ego enters the room. Because subtle power doesn't announce itself, it is easy to dismiss. A negotiator may interrupt the junior team member who is actually the architect of the recommendation. They may disregard a project manager's hesitation without realizing that person controls operational follow-through. Power that doesn't look like power is often underestimated precisely because it is not loud.

Another danger is misreading civility as weakness. The calm participant who asks clarifying questions may not be passive, they may be gathering information. The person who speaks least may be the one whose opinion carries the most weight afterward. Overlooking subtle power creates blind spots. And blind spots create surprise.

The Pointer

Map influence, not just authority.

If you want to negotiate effectively, map the ecosystem, not just the organizational chart. Before entering a negotiation, ask:

- Who shapes this person's thinking?
- Who prepares their information?
- Who must live with the consequences of this decision?
- Who can slow implementation?
- Who has informal credibility others defer to?

This is mapping influence. In construction settings, this may mean understanding that the foreman's buy-in determines whether a schedule adjustment works in practice. In labor negotiations, it may mean recognizing that the rank-and-file sentiment influences whether leadership can sell the agreement. In executive settings, it may mean realizing that a long-tenured advisor holds more sway than a newly appointed vice president.

The pointer is simple: Treat quiet power with the same seriousness as visible authority. Engage it early. Respect it publicly. Seek its perspective privately. Instead of asking only, "Who decides?" also ask, "Who shapes the decision?" When you identify subtle power, you can work with it rather than collide with it.

That may mean briefing influencers before formal meetings. It may mean validating operational concerns before finalizing language. It may mean ensuring that those who implement an agreement feel heard before it is signed. Power that doesn't look like power is often relational. It grows from trust and credibility built over time. And unlike formal authority, it cannot be demanded, it must be earned.

The most effective negotiators do not attempt to overpower a system. They align with its real influence patterns. In the end, visible authority may sign the agreement. But invisible power often determines whether it was possible in the first place. Learn to see it. Respect it and engage it.

CHAPTER FOUR

MANAGING CONFLICT IN MOTION

"Experienced negotiators understand that once threats are public, retreat becomes expensive."

INSIGHT 30 – CONFLICT IS DATA

Most people experience conflict as disruption. Noise. Irritation. A breakdown in cooperation. Seasoned negotiators experience it differently. They experience it as information.

Conflict is not random. It does not appear out of nowhere. It emerges when expectations collide, when incentives misalign, when identity feels threatened, or when risk is distributed unevenly. If you learn to read it instead of reacting to it, conflict becomes one of the most valuable diagnostic tools available to you.

The problem is not that conflict exists. The problem is that most people misinterpret what it's telling them.

The Principle

Conflict reveals what matters.

When tension rises, something important is being touched.

Conflict reveals:

- Where perceived loss is greater than perceived gain.
- Where values or identity feel at risk.
- Where incentives are misaligned.
- Where communication has broken down.
- Where power dynamics are being tested.

People escalate when something they care about feels threatened. The louder the reaction, the more data you are being given.

Consider a project meeting where a superintendent pushes back hard on a schedule revision. On the surface, it looks like resistance to change. But beneath that resistance might be:

- Fear of losing credibility with the crew.
- Concern about safety shortcuts.
- Fatigue from prior compressed timelines.
- Pressure from upstream trades.
- Distrust from previous unfulfilled promises.

If you argue the schedule harder, you are arguing the symptom. If you analyze the conflict, you are diagnosing the system. Conflict tells you where pressure is building. When someone says “this is unacceptable,” what they often mean is “Something important to me feels exposed.” Emotion is not the problem. It is a signal.

In negotiation theory, this is the distinction between positions and interests, a concept widely popularized by the book Getting to Yes by Roger Fisher and William Ury.

Positions are the visible argument. Interests are the invisible drivers. Conflict is the flare in the sky that tells you where the real issue lives.

The Pitfall

Treating conflict as a threat instead of information.

Most people are conditioned to neutralize conflict as quickly as possible. They smooth it over, they dominate it, they avoid it and they shut it down.

All of those reactions share a common assumption: conflict is danger. And sometimes it is. But more often, it is feedback. When you treat conflict as a threat, you respond defensively. You argue harder. You raise your voice. You tighten your posture. You counterattack and the data disappears.

Once people feel dismissed or overpowered, they stop revealing what truly matters. They retreat into rigid positions. They protect themselves. Now you are negotiating against armor instead of insight.

On a jobsite, imagine a subcontractor repeatedly missing coordination meetings. The project manager confronts him publicly. The subcontractor snaps back, "We're doing the best we can." The meeting becomes a power contest.

What was missed? Perhaps the subcontractor is understaffed. Perhaps change orders are overwhelming his back office. Perhaps he feels disrespected by sequencing decisions made without his input. If you shut him down to restore order, you restore silence not alignment. Silence is not agreement. It is suppressed data.

When leaders equate calm with health, they often miss the warning signs. Systems under stress produce friction. Removing the friction without diagnosing the stress only delays the breakdown. The pitfall is confusing the presence of conflict with failure. In reality, the absence of visible conflict can signal disengagement, resentment, or resignation, which are far more expensive in the long run.

The Pointer

Slow down and ask, "What is this teaching me?"

The disciplined move in conflict is not escalation. It is curiosity.

When tension rises, ask yourself:

- What does the intensity tell me?
- What risk is this person trying to avoid?
- What identity feels threatened?
- What constraint am I not seeing?
- Where might incentives be misaligned?

Then ask them calmly, "Help me understand what concerns you most about this." That single sentence shifts conflict from combat to diagnosis. You are not conceding. You are gathering intelligence. The goal is not to eliminate disagreement. The goal is to surface the underlying drivers before they harden into hostility. Sometimes the data will confirm you need to hold the line. Sometimes it will reveal you are missing something critical. Either way, you are operating from awareness instead of reaction.

Well managed conflict builds credibility and it unlocks the creative genius in people. When they feel heard, even if they don't get everything they want, it reduces defensive escalation. Over time, teams learn that tension is not punished, it is examined. That culture transforms conflict from personal attack into problem-solving fuel.

The seasoned negotiator understands something subtle: Conflict is not the opposite of cooperation. Unexamined conflict is.

When you treat friction as feedback, you stop fearing it.

You start reading it. And when you read it well, you make better decisions, about people, about risk, and about timing. Conflict is not noise. It is data. The question is whether you are disciplined enough to analyze it before you try to silence it.

INSIGHT 31 - EARLY SIGNS OF ESCALATION

Escalation rarely begins with shouting. It begins with subtle shifts - tone tightening, position hardening, curiosity shrinking. By the time a negotiation explodes, the early warning lights have usually been blinking for some time. Seasoned negotiators learn to spot these signals early, when intervention is still possible and dignity is still intact.

The skill is not merely conflict management. It is conflict detection.

The Principle

Escalation is a process, not an event.

Escalation does not arrive all at once. It builds in stages. The first stage is almost always psychological before it becomes behavioral. Watch for these early markers:

- Language narrows. Words like "always," "never," and "non-negotiable" begin to appear.
- Questions decrease. Statements replace inquiry.
- Positions harden. People repeat the same demand instead of exploring alternatives.
- Tone shifts. Volume may not increase, but sharpness does.
- Face becomes central. The discussion subtly moves from "What works?" to "Who's right?"

At this stage, nothing dramatic has happened. No one has stormed out. No ultimatums have been issued. But the temperature has changed. Escalation is often fueled by three psychological triggers:

1. Perceived disrespect.
2. Loss of control.
3. Threat to identity or status.

When someone feels dismissed, cornered, or diminished, the negotiation quietly transitions from problem-solving to self-protection. And once self-protection takes over, flexibility disappears.

The experienced negotiator treats these early signals as diagnostic data, not irritations. A tightening jaw, crossed arms, or a repeated phrase is not a nuisance, it is an indicator that pressure is building somewhere beneath the surface. If you wait for raised voices, you are already late.

The Pitfall

Responding to escalation with counter-escalation.

The most common mistake is reflexive mirroring.

- Tone sharpens - You sharpen.
- Positions harden - You harden.
- Accusation appears - You defend.

This feels natural. It feels strong. It feels justified. But it is also gasoline on a spark. When escalation begins, most people interpret it as aggression rather than anxiety. They assume intent rather than insecurity. And they respond with firmness instead of curiosity. The result is predictable:

- Conversations become binary.
- Options shrink.
- Saving face overtakes solving problems.
- Both parties feel unheard.

Another common error is ignoring the signals altogether. Some negotiators attempt to “power through” the discomfort. They push harder on logic, numbers, or contract language, believing facts will calm emotion. They rarely do. Facts are rarely persuasive when identity feels threatened. The longer early escalation goes unaddressed, the more likely it is to transform into:

- Personal attacks.
- Public posturing.
- Formal grievances.
- Walkouts or ultimatums.

By then, resolution becomes more expensive - emotionally, relationally, and sometimes financially. Escalation thrives on unattended tension.

The Pointer

Intervene early - lower the temperature before solving the problem.

The key to managing escalation is timing. The earlier you intervene, the lighter the touch required. There are four practical moves that seasoned negotiators use when they detect early escalation:

1. Name the Shift Without Blame.

You might say: "It feels like we're starting to dig in a bit. Can we pause for a moment?" This does two things:

- It surfaces the tension without accusation.
- It resets the emotional frame without attacking anyone's position.

Naming tension often diffuses it.

2. Shift from Position to Concern.

If someone says, "That's unacceptable," resist debating the label. Instead ask: "What's your biggest concern with it?" This redirects the conversation from a rigid stance to the underlying interest. Escalation lives in positions. Resolution lives in concerns.

3. Slow the Pace

Escalation accelerates tempo. People talk faster, they interrupt more and decide quicker. Consciously slow the rhythm. Lower your voice and increase pauses. Ask one question at a time. Calm is contagious, but only if someone models it first.

4. Protect Face

If identity or status feels threatened, look for ways to affirm competence or intent. "I know you've been trying to protect your team on this."

That single sentence can restore dignity and reopen flexibility.

Escalation often recedes when people feel seen.

The most powerful negotiators are not those who dominate a room. They are those who detect invisible shifts. They notice:

- The moment curiosity turns into certainty.
- The instant collaboration shifts into competition.
- The point where solving the issue becomes secondary to winning the exchange.

These are the hinge moments. If you intervene there, gently and deliberately, you preserve options. If you miss them, you inherit damage control. The goal is not to suppress disagreement. Disagreement is healthy. The goal is to prevent disagreement from mutating into identity conflict. Early signs of escalation are not warnings that the negotiation is failing. They are invitations to lead. When you treat tension as data, respond with composure instead of ego, and intervene before the room heats up, you do more than avoid conflict, you build credibility.

The negotiator who can lower the temperature earns something far more valuable than a single concession, they earn trust. And trust, once established in the early tremors of escalation, often prevents the earthquake entirely.

INSIGHT 32 – THE ESCALATION LADDER

Conflict rarely explodes without warning. It climbs. What looks like a sudden blow-up is usually the final rung of a ladder people have been ascending for days, weeks, sometimes months. The raised voice, the threatening email, the walkout from the meeting,

these are not beginnings. They are late-stage symptoms.

Seasoned negotiators understand escalation as a predictable progression. And if it progresses in steps, it can be interrupted in steps.

The Principle

Escalation is incremental - not instant.

Escalation follows a pattern. It typically moves through recognizable stages:

1. Internal Reaction - Frustration, suspicion, irritation. Nothing said yet, but emotion is building.
2. Interpretation -"They're disrespecting me." "They're trying to take advantage." Motives are assigned.
3. Position Hardening - Language shifts from flexible to rigid. "We can't do that." "That's unacceptable."
4. Personalization - The issue becomes about identity, ego, competence, or authority.
5. Public Commitment - Statements are made in front of others. Email chains widen. Lines get drawn.
6. Threats or Ultimatums - "Take it or leave it." "We'll see you in court." "I'll escalate this."

Each rung makes it harder to climb back down. Not because solutions disappear, but because pride, audience, and emotion make retreat feel like defeat.

On a construction site, this might begin with a schedule disagreement. A superintendent questions a delay explanation. A project manager interprets that as a challenge to competence. Emails copy senior leadership. Suddenly, what started as a sequencing issue becomes a reputational battle. The ladder wasn't visible, but it was there. The seasoned negotiator watches for rungs, not explosions.

The Pitfall

Treating every rung like the top.

The most common mistake is responding to early-stage tension with late-stage force. A mild frustration is met with legal language. A tentative complaint is met with formal documentation. A scheduling concern is met with a contractual threat. This response accelerates the climb.

When someone is on rung two, interpreting intent, and you respond as if they are on rung six, issuing ultimatums, you validate their suspicion that this is adversarial. You collapse the ladder upward.

Another pitfall is waiting too long. Leaders often ignore early tension because "it's minor." They hope it will burn out. But unaddressed frustration rarely disappears; it compounds. Silence allows interpretation to harden into narrative. By the time formal escalation occurs, both sides believe the other has been unreasonable for weeks. At that point, solving the technical issue is easy. Repairing the relationship is not. Escalation feels dramatic at the top, but it is decided at the bottom.

The Pointer

Intervene one rung below the heat.

The key to managing the escalation ladder is simple: respond one level below the visible intensity. If someone is rigid, introduce curiosity. If someone is emotional, introduce calm. If someone is threatening, introduce structure. Never match intensity with equal intensity. That is how ladders turn into cliffs.

Here are three practical interventions:

1. Name the Rung. When you sense position hardening, say: "It sounds like this issue has more weight than just schedule. Help me understand what's at risk for you." This interrupts interpretation before it becomes personalization.
2. Move the Forum. Escalation thrives in public settings. Pride grows with audience size. If tension is rising in a group meeting, suggest a smaller conversation. "Let's step aside for five minutes and sort this out."

Removing the audience lowers the cost of flexibility.

3. Separate Issue from Identity. When the conflict becomes personal, deliberately re-anchor it in the problem. "This isn't about whether your team is competent. It's about sequencing risk on level three. Let's solve that." Identity is gasoline. Issues are solvable.

Escalation is not always accidental. Sometimes it is tactical. Parties may escalate to gain leverage, create urgency, or force executive attention. A subcontractor may threaten delay claims to accelerate payment. A union representative may raise public pressure to strengthen bargaining position. But even strategic escalation obeys the ladder. It still carries risk.

Once threats are public, retreat becomes expensive. Once legal counsel enters, flexibility narrows. Once leadership is involved, face becomes central. Experienced negotiators use escalation carefully and rarely. They understand that climbing is easy; descending is hard.

De-escalation requires deliberate action:

- Slow the tempo.
- Narrow the audience.
- Clarify intent.
- Restore optionality.

Often, it begins with a simple reset: "Let's pause. I don't think this is serving either of us. What outcome are we actually trying to protect here?" This question shifts attention from winning the rung to solving the problem.

The Escalation Ladder teaches a critical truth: conflict rarely surprises those who are paying attention. Every harsh ultimatum began as a quiet frustration. Every legal threat began as a private interpretation. Every broken relationship began with a small, unattended slight.

The seasoned negotiator does not wait for explosions. They watch the climb. They intervene early. And when necessary, they build a way down before anyone reaches the top.

INSIGHT 33 – INTERRUPTING THE CONFLICT SPIRAL

Conflict rarely explodes without warning. It spirals.

A comment is misunderstood. A tone is misread. A delay is interpreted as disrespect. One side hardens. The other pushes back. Positions become sharper, language becomes tighter, and soon the original issue is buried beneath reaction.

Escalation is not a single moment. It is a sequence. Seasoned negotiators understand that the key to managing conflict is not winning at the top of the spiral - it is interrupting it early, before gravity takes over.

The Principle

Escalation is a process - and processes can be disrupted.

Conflict operates like a tightening coil. Each move triggers a counter-move. Each reaction justifies the next reaction. The spiral feeds on speed, certainty, and ego.

Interrupting the spiral requires recognizing that what feels personal is often structural. The spiral is fueled by three accelerants:

- Assumed intent ("They're doing this on purpose.")
- Public positioning ("I've already taken a stand.")
- Reciprocal escalation ("If they push, I push back harder.")

Left alone, this dynamic becomes self-reinforcing. The louder one side becomes, the more the other side believes escalation is necessary. Interrupting the spiral does not mean surrendering. It means changing the pattern.

The most effective interrupters do three things:

1. They slow the tempo. Speed is the ally of escalation. Slowing down - through a pause, a clarifying question, or even a reframing statement - weakens the spiral's momentum.
2. They shift from accusation to analysis. Instead of debating who is right, they examine what is happening. "We seem to be getting further apart. Let's reset."
3. They separate identity from issue. Spirals intensify when people feel attacked. Re-centering the discussion on the problem reduces the threat response.

The spiral depends on reflex. Interruption depends on intention.

The Pitfall

Fighting harder when you feel threatened.

The most common mistake in escalation is instinctive retaliation. When challenged, most people escalate one level above what they just received. A sharp comment gets a sharper reply. A rigid demand meets an ultimatum. Each side believes it is merely defending itself. But escalation is rarely symmetrical. It compounds.

The pitfall is believing strength equals force. In reality, force often deepens the spiral.

Another common error is misdiagnosing silence as weakness. Sometimes when someone withdraws, it is not surrender, it is calculation. If you interpret withdrawal as victory and press harder, you may trigger a more dramatic counter-escalation later.

On a construction project, for example, a superintendent publicly challenges a subcontractor's timeline. The subcontractor responds defensively. The superintendent tightens oversight. The subcontractor slows cooperation. Soon, what began as a scheduling conversation becomes a power struggle.

Each side believes the other started it. No one pauses long enough to interrupt it. The spiral thrives when both parties are more committed to being right than being effective.

The Pointer

Name the pattern, change the pattern.

To interrupt the spiral, you must first see it and then name it without blame. Simple pattern-interrupting phrases can reset momentum:

- "I think we're starting to dig in. Let's take a breath."

- "We both want this resolved. Let's shift how we're talking about it."
- "Before we go further, what outcome are we actually trying to achieve?"

These are not soft statements. They are strategic ones.

Another powerful interrupt is curiosity. Genuine questions slow the brain's defensive circuitry. Instead of countering a demand, explore it:

- "Help me understand what's driving that concern."
- "What would success look like from your perspective?"

Questions reintroduce thought where reaction has taken over. Tone matters as much as content. Calm delivery under pressure is contagious. Escalation is emotional mimicry; interruption is emotional leadership.

Timing also matters. Early interruption requires less energy. Waiting until voices rise and reputations are publicly staked makes resetting more costly.

Finally, consider private versus public correction. Spirals accelerate when audiences are present. If possible, step aside. Removing the crowd removes the need to perform. Interrupting the spiral is not about avoiding tension. It is about redirecting it before it calcifies.

Every negotiation contains moments where the spiral begins to form. The seasoned negotiator does not deny these moments. They anticipate them.

They watch for subtle cues:

- Increased speed in speech.
- More absolute language. ("always," "never")
- Diminished listening.
- Hardening body language.

These are early signals of tightening dynamics.

Interruption is an act of leadership because it requires absorbing a moment of discomfort. Someone must resist the urge to retaliate. Someone must choose to pause when pushing feels more natural.

That choice changes the trajectory. Conflict spirals because both sides react automatically. It stabilizes when one side acts deliberately. The strongest negotiator in the room is not the one who can escalate most convincingly. It is the one who can step outside the pattern and reset it.

Interrupting the spiral is not about winning the exchange. It is about protecting the relationship, the objective, and the long-term outcome.

Escalation feels powerful in the moment. Interruption is powerful in the long run.

INSIGHT 34 – REPRESENTATION WITHOUT PROVOCATION

One of the quiet disciplines of effective negotiation is the ability to represent interests firmly without provoking unnecessary resistance. In many disputes, especially those involving strong personalities, high stakes, or public visibility, the way an argument

is delivered can matter as much as the substance of the argument itself. Skilled negotiators understand that their role is not simply to advocate, but to advocate in a way that keeps the conversation productive rather than combustible.

Representation without provocation begins with understanding the difference between clarity and aggression. Clarity communicates position, reasoning, and priorities in a way that others can understand and respond to. Aggression, on the other hand, often seeks to overpower rather than persuade. When people feel attacked, cornered, or publicly challenged, their natural response is rarely cooperation. More often it is defensiveness, entrenchment, or retaliation. What could have been a difficult but manageable discussion quickly becomes a contest of pride.

In negotiation, representation is unavoidable. Whether you are a superintendent speaking for ownership, a union steward speaking for the crew, or a project executive speaking for investors, you carry more than your own voice. You carry authority, expectations, and often frustration that predates you.

The challenge is this: how do you represent firmly without provoking unnecessarily?

The Principle

Strength does not require sharp edges.

Effective representation is clear, steady, and anchored in legitimacy - not volume.

When you represent a client or organization, your job is not to intimidate the other side. It is to articulate boundaries, standards, and constraints in a way that can be heard. The moment representation turns theatrical - raised voices, exaggerated ultimatums, dramatic exits - you stop representing interests and start provoking identity. Provocation invites counter-provocation. And once ego enters the room, clarity leaves.

Consider high-level labor negotiations during the formation of the National Labor Relations Board in the 1930s. The most effective representatives on both sides were not the loudest. They were the ones who could say, calmly, "Here is what my side must have, and here is why." They framed their demands as structural realities, not personal attacks.

Representation without provocation requires three disciplines:

1. Clarity of mandate - Know exactly what you can and cannot move.
2. Neutral tone - State boundaries without contempt.
3. Separation of message from emotion - Deliver firm content without emotional escalation.

Calm firmness often feels more powerful than aggression. When someone states, "We cannot accept that term. It violates our insurance requirements," If said without anger, the message lands as policy, not defiance.

Calm communicates control. Control communicates strength, and strength that does not threaten is easier to negotiate with.

The Pitfall

Confusing toughness with aggression.

Many negotiators believe they must "show strength" early. They posture. They anchor with extreme demands. They interrupt. They signal dominance. What they are actually doing is triggering defense mechanisms.

The human nervous system does not parse subtle distinctions. It reacts to threat. When representation sounds like accusation, such as "You're being unreasonable," or "You're out of line," or "You're not negotiating in good faith," the other side stops processing content and starts protecting identity.

This is where escalation begins.

We see this pattern repeatedly in international diplomacy. During early Cold War exchanges between the United States and the Soviet Union, public rhetoric often hardened positions unnecessarily. Leaders sometimes boxed themselves in with provocative language designed for domestic audiences. Once words were spoken publicly, backing down became politically costly even if private channels were more flexible. Provocation narrows options.

In everyday negotiations, the dynamic is the same. A project manager says, "That's ridiculous," and now the other side must defend their intelligence. A union rep says, "You're exploiting the workforce," and management must defend its integrity. Neither statement advances substance. Both inflame identity. The pitfall is believing that aggression equals leverage.

In reality, aggression often reduces leverage because it reduces flexibility. The other side becomes less willing to collaborate, not because your interests are invalid, but because your delivery made them feel attacked. Provocation may feel satisfying in the moment. It rarely produces durable agreements.

The Pointer

Represent the constraint, not the contempt.

The practical move is this: when delivering a hard message, shift from accusation to constraint.

- Instead of: “You’re asking too much.”
- Say: “That number exceeds our budget ceiling.”
- Instead of: “That’s not acceptable.”
- Say: “We don’t have authority to approve that term.”

Notice the difference. The first version assigns blame. The second version assigns structure.

This technique works because it redirects pressure away from personal confrontation and toward external realities, policy, budget, timeline, regulation, and precedent. You are not saying “I refuse.” You are saying “The structure prevents this.”

This approach mirrors how seasoned litigators and negotiators present arguments before bodies like the United States Supreme Court. The most persuasive advocates do not attack opposing counsel personally. They anchor arguments in statute, precedent, and constitutional interpretation. The authority lies in structure, not in volume.

In your world - whether construction, labor relations, or executive deal making - the same principle applies. When voices rise, lower yours. When accusations appear, return to standards. When pressure mounts, slow the tempo.

You can even make your representation explicit by saying: “I’m not questioning your authority, I’m counting on it,” or “I want to be clear. I’m not challenging your intent. I’m explaining the constraint I’m operating under.” Those sentences alone can de-escalate an exchange.

Another powerful pointer is to preview firmness before

delivering it: "I'm going to say something that may be difficult to hear, but it's important for clarity." This signals strength without hostility. It prepares the nervous system on the other side to receive the message.

Representation without provocation is not passive. It is disciplined. It requires emotional control, precision of language, and awareness of how quickly identity threats derail substance. The seasoned negotiator understands something subtle - you can defend your side completely without attacking theirs. And when you do, two things happen.

First, you preserve the working relationship. Second, you preserve room to move. In negotiation, room to move is power.

Representation without provocation is not about being soft. It is about being strategic enough to know that the goal is agreement, not victory theater. Strength, delivered calmly, is rarely resisted. It is respected.

INSIGHT 35 – SPEAKING FOR YOUR PEOPLE WITHOUT BURNING THE BRIDGE

In construction, labor relations, executive leadership, or project management, there comes a moment when you are no longer speaking only for yourself. You are speaking for your crew, your department, your company or your members. And that changes everything.

When you carry others' concerns into the room, emotion rides with you, expectations ride with you and sometimes anger rides with you. The danger is clear: in trying to prove loyalty to your side, you unintentionally torch the relationship with the other side.

Representing your people does not require burning the bridge with the other side. In fact, the more effectively you carry the voice of your side, the more carefully you must protect the working relationship across the table. The art lies in advocating firmly while preserving the conditions that make agreement possible.

Many negotiators misinterpret advocacy as confrontation. They assume that to demonstrate loyalty to their side they must escalate language, harden positions, or signal unwavering resistance. The performance of toughness becomes a substitute for the discipline of representation. Unfortunately, that performance often produces the opposite result.

Strong representation and durable relationships are not

opposites. But they require discipline. How do you advocate fiercely without creating enemies you'll have to negotiate with again next month?

The Principle

Represent interests, not outrage.

The first responsibility of a representative is clarity. When your people send you into the room, they usually send you with positions:

- "We're not accepting that schedule."
- "We want more manpower."
- "That pay structure is unacceptable."
- "We're tired of being ignored."

But beneath every position is an interest. Beneath every complaint is a fear, a pressure, or a constraint. If you simply amplify the outrage, you escalate the conflict. If you translate the outrage into structured interests, you elevate the conversation.

- Saying: My team is furious about this, feels loyal.
- But saying: My team is concerned about safety exposure and burnout if the schedule remains unchanged, is leadership.

One inflames. The other clarifies.

When you represent interests instead of emotion, three things happen:

1. You maintain credibility with the other side.
2. You reduce defensiveness.
3. You increase the likelihood of problem-solving.

Strong advocates do not water down concerns. They refine them. You are not there to vent. You are there to convert pressure into productive dialogue.

The Pitfall

Confusing aggression with loyalty.

Many leaders fall into a trap: they believe that unless they speak sharply, threaten strongly, or escalate visibly, their people will think they are weak.

So, they pound the table. They use phrases like:

"This is non-negotiable."

"We won't tolerate this."

"You need to fix this immediately."

"This is unacceptable."

They walk out. They escalate. They draw hard lines publicly. It may feel powerful in the moment. It may earn applause from their side afterward.

But what it often does is burn quiet bridges:

- The other side becomes less willing to share information.
- Trust erodes.
- Future concessions shrink.
- The relationship becomes transactional instead of strategic.

And here's the deeper danger: when you consistently escalate to prove loyalty, you create expectations of escalation. Your people start to believe force is the only language that works.

Now every disagreement requires heat. Over time, you trap yourself. If you try to be measured later, your own side may see it as weakness. The seasoned negotiator understands something critical: You can be firm without being inflammatory. You can be resolute without being hostile. You can be loyal without being reckless. Burning the bridge might feel like strength—but it reduces your leverage tomorrow.

The Pointer

Use the "dual commitment" frame.

When you speak for your people, anchor your message in two commitments simultaneously:

1. Commitment to your people's legitimate interests.
2. Commitment to the ongoing working relationship. Say both. Explicitly.

For example: "I have a responsibility to make sure my team isn't put in a position that increases safety risk. That's non-negotiable for me. At the same time, we've worked well together before, and I want to find a solution that keeps this project moving." That structure changes the energy in the room. You're not attacking. You're not retreating. You're aligning firmness with continuity.

Another variation: "My people need predictability on this issue. I'm not going to ignore that. But I'm also not interested in turning this into a standoff. Let's work through the constraints." Notice what happens:

- You validate your side.
- You avoid vilifying the other side.
- You keep the bridge intact.

The "dual commitment" frame signals maturity. It reassures your people that you're not backing down. It reassures the other side that you're not declaring war. And that balance preserves influence.

Sometimes your people are angrier than you are. They want you to "send a message." They want visible toughness.

This is where leadership becomes containment. You can acknowledge their frustration privately without carrying their anger publicly.

You can say to your team: "I understand the frustration. I'm going to address this firmly. But I'm not going to damage relationships we still need." That transparency protects you internally while preserving bridges externally. If you lose the relationship, your people lose leverage. Strong representation requires emotional discipline.

In industries like construction, where the same contractors, labor leaders, superintendents, and executives see each other again and again, the negotiation never truly ends. Today's opponent may be tomorrow's partner. Today's conflict may be next quarter's collaboration.

Burning a bridge rarely produces lasting victories. Speaking for your people without burning the bridge means:

- Translating emotion into interests.
- Demonstrating firmness without hostility.
- Making dual commitments visible.
- Playing the long game, not the emotional moment.

The strongest representatives are not the loudest. They are the most controlled. They understand that power is not displayed through destruction. It is demonstrated through disciplined advocacy that protects both the people you serve - and the relationships you still need.

INSIGHT 36 – INTERNAL ALIGNMENT BEFORE EXTERNAL NEGOTIATION

Negotiation does not begin across the table. It begins behind closed doors.

Seasoned negotiators understand a truth that is often overlooked by less experienced leaders: many negotiations fail long before anyone sits across the table. They fail internally. External negotiation is only as effective as the clarity, discipline, and alignment behind it. When the people on your side are uncertain about objectives, divided on priorities, or inconsistent in their messaging, the other party will sense it almost immediately. Misalignment inside the organization quietly becomes leverage for the other side.

Internal alignment means ensuring that everyone representing your interests understands three things clearly: what outcome matters most, what flexibility exists, and what boundaries cannot be crossed. Without this clarity, negotiators improvise under pressure.

Before proposals are drafted, before positions are declared, before anyone says "we need to talk," a quieter negotiation is already underway, inside your own organization. The quality of that internal alignment will determine the quality of everything that follows.

Deals collapse far more often from internal fracture than from external opposition. If your team is divided, unclear, or quietly resistant, the other side will sense it, and leverage it.

The Principle

Unity is leverage.

External strength is a reflection of internal clarity. Alignment does not mean unanimous agreement. It means shared understanding. Your team must be clear on:

- What outcome are we seeking?
- What problem are we actually trying to solve?
- What are we willing to concede and what is non-negotiable?
- Who has decision authority?
- What is our walk-away point?

Without those answers, negotiation becomes improvisation under pressure.

In many organizations, the external negotiator is sent forward with incomplete authority, vague guardrails, and conflicting stakeholder expectations. The negotiator then carries an invisible burden: translating between factions inside while simultaneously negotiating outside. That is not leverage. That is vulnerability.

When internal alignment is strong, three things happen:

1. Messaging becomes consistent. The other side hears the same story from every representative.
2. Decisions happen faster. There is no constant retreat to "check with the team."
3. Confidence rises. The negotiator speaks from mandate, not hesitation.

Alignment is not about control; it is about coherence. Coherence builds credibility. Credibility builds influence. If your organization cannot agree internally on what it wants, the other side will define the outcome for you.

The Pitfall

Mistaking silence for agreement.

The most dangerous internal misalignment is the quiet one. Leaders often assume alignment because no one openly objects. But silence is not consent. Silence is often:

- Deference to hierarchy.
- Fear of conflict.
- Political caution.
- Fatigue.
- Or quiet disagreement waiting for leverage.

When internal dissent is suppressed rather than revealed, it resurfaces later - at the worst possible moment. A senior executive nods in planning meetings but later signals doubt to the other side. A project manager agrees to terms but privately believes they are unrealistic. A stakeholder feels excluded and withholds cooperation during implementation. The negotiation may appear successful externally, yet unravel internally.

Another common mistake is confusing strategy discussion with alignment work. If teams debate tactics, anchoring numbers, sequencing issues, and timing proposals, without first resolving fundamental differences about risk tolerance, relationship priorities, or long-term objectives they are subject to a strategy of fragmentation. The negotiator then becomes a courier of mixed messages. The other side senses hesitation, inconsistency, or shifting positions. They probe. They exploit. They divide. Nothing weakens negotiating power more than visible internal disagreement.

The Pointer

Conduct the alignment conversation explicitly.

Alignment does not happen organically. It must be engineered. Before stepping into any significant negotiation, hold an intentional internal alignment session. Not a briefing. Not a status update. A structured alignment conversation.

Ask, and answer, clearly:

1. What does success look like specifically? Define outcomes in measurable terms. Vague goals create later conflict.
2. What trade-offs are acceptable? Price versus timeline. Control versus flexibility. Short-term gain versus long-term positioning.
3. Where are we divided? Surface disagreement openly. Encourage dissent. Pressure-test assumptions internally so they are not exposed externally.
4. Who decides in the moment? Clarify authority boundaries. A negotiator who must pause for every decision is signaling weakness.
5. What story are we telling? Alignment is not only about numbers. It is about narrative. The story your organization tells must be consistent across departments and representatives.

Encourage constructive tension internally. The negotiation table is not the place to discover that your own team sees the deal differently.

Another powerful alignment tool is pre-mortem thinking. Ask the team: "It's six months from now and this deal failed. Why?" The answers will reveal hidden doubts and structural weaknesses before they become reality.

Finally, assign a single point of synthesis. Someone must integrate internal perspectives into a coherent strategy.

Without synthesis, alignment conversations become circular debates. Alignment is not achieved when everyone feels comfortable. It is achieved when everyone understands and commits.

External negotiation is theater. Internal alignment is architecture. The audience sees the performance, but the structure beneath determines whether it stands. Skilled negotiators understand that their first responsibility is not persuasion - it is preparation. Not of slides, not of talking points, but of people.

When your internal stakeholders are aligned:

- You move decisively.
- You speak consistently.
- You concede strategically.
- You hold firm confidently. When they are not:
- You hesitate.
- You contradict yourself.
- You overpromise.
- You fracture under pressure.

Before you negotiate with them, negotiate with yourselves. Because unity is quiet power — and quiet power is difficult to defeat.

INSIGHT 37 – ORID AND STRUCTURED DIALOGUE UNDER PRESSURE

In high-pressure negotiations, conversation often becomes reactive, fragmented, and emotionally charged. People speak past one another, arguments spiral, and the discussion shifts from solving a problem to defending identity. What experienced negotiators

understand is that productive dialogue rarely happens by accident - especially under pressure. It must be structured.

Pressure compresses thinking.

On a job-site, in a boardroom, across a bargaining table, when tension rises, cognition narrows. People skip steps. They jump to conclusions. They argue opinions as if they were facts. Structured dialogue is not a luxury in those moments. It is a stabilizer.

One of the most practical frameworks for structured conversation under pressure is known as ORID Protocols: Objective, Reflective, Interpretive, and Decisional questions. It is deceptively simple. And precisely because it is simple, it works when stress is high.

While it originated as a facilitation practice ORID is not a trick, it is a discipline.

The Principle

Structure slows escalation.

ORID imposes sequence on chaos. When conflict heats up, conversations usually leap from raw data straight to decision, or worse, from emotion straight to accusation. ORID restores order by guiding the dialogue through four deliberate stages:

1. Objective - What are the facts? What actually happened? What was said? What numbers are we looking at? What timelines are real?
2. Reflective - What are we feeling or reacting to? What surprised us? What concerns us? What feels risky? What is frustrating?
3. Interpretive - What does this mean? What are the implications? What are the risks? What patterns are emerging? What assumptions might we be making?
4. Decisional - What will we do? What are our options? What is the next step? Who is responsible? By when?

Under pressure, people tend to compress these stages into one emotionally charged exchange. ORID separates them.

When you force a group to stay in the Objective stage before interpreting, you reduce distortion. When you legitimize the Reflective stage, you prevent emotion from hijacking the Interpretive stage. When you move deliberately to Decisional, you avoid premature commitments driven by anxiety.

Structure reduces reactivity. In high-stakes negotiations, this sequencing does three critical things:

1. It lowers defensiveness by clarifying facts before blame.
2. It surfaces emotion without allowing it to dominate.

3. It ensures decisions are built on shared understanding, not competing narratives.

The seasoned negotiator understands that structure is not rigidity. It is scaffolding. Under pressure, it provides a stable, secure platform for working.

The Pitfall

Using structure as a weapon.

Structure can calm a room, or inflame it. The most common mistake with ORID is using it mechanically or manipulatively. When someone rigidly "facilitates" while others are emotionally charged, it can feel patronizing.

"Let's stay in the Objective phase." "We're not at interpretation yet." "Let's table feelings for later." If tone and timing are wrong, the structure feels like control rather than clarity.

Another mistake is skipping the Reflective stage because it feels uncomfortable. Leaders often want to move straight from facts to analysis. But suppressed emotion doesn't disappear; it leaks. It shows up as sarcasm, resistance, or passive sabotage.

A third pitfall is confusing interpretation with fact. Groups frequently believe they are in the Objective stage when they are actually arguing Interpretations:

"That subcontractor is unreliable." (Interpretation.) "They missed three deadlines in the last month." (Objective.)

If the Objective stage is polluted with judgments, the entire structure weakens.

Under pressure, people also rush the Decisional phase. They want relief. A quick decision feels like progress. But a decision built on incomplete interpretation often creates a second conflict downstream.

Structure must be held lightly but firmly. It is a guide, not a script.

The Pointer

Lead the sequence, not the outcome.

The power of ORID is not in controlling what people conclude. It is in controlling how they think together. When tension is rising, try this: Start with calm clarity. “Before we jump to solutions, let’s make sure we agree on what actually happened.”

Anchor the Objective stage with specific, neutral questions:

- What was the original scope?
- What changed?
- What does the contract say?

What are the current numbers?

- Then intentionally invite the Reflective stage:
- What concerns you most about this?
- What feels unfair?
- What risk are you worried about?

This is where pressure often diffuses. When people feel heard, volume drops.

Next, guide the Interpretive stage:

- What does this pattern suggest?
- If we continue like this, what happens in 60 days?
- What assumptions might we be making about each other?

Notice that these questions elevate thinking. They shift the group from reaction to analysis.

Only then move to Decisional:

- What are two workable paths forward?

- What are we prepared to commit to today?
- What needs further analysis before commitment?

The seasoned negotiator does not rush this progression. They pace it. Under severe pressure, tight deadlines, public scrutiny, or financial exposure this sequencing becomes even more valuable. The greater the stress, the more disciplined the structure must be.

But here is the deeper pointer - use ORID internally before you use it externally.

When you feel your own pulse rising, ask yourself:

- What are the objective facts?
- What am I reacting to emotionally?
- What meaning am I assigning to this?
- What decision do I actually want to make?

Self-structure precedes group structure. ORID is not a meeting technique. It is a thinking discipline. Under pressure, the loudest voice often wins. Structured dialogue ensures the clearest thinking wins instead.

In negotiation, clarity is leverage. Structure is how you protect it.

INSIGHT 38 – DEALING WITH PUBLIC POSTURING

There is a particular tension that enters a negotiation the moment it goes public.

It may be a press release, a social media post, a speech at a union hall, a memo copied to half the organization, or a carefully worded statement to stakeholders. Once positions are declared publicly, the temperature changes. What might have been a problem-solving conversation becomes a stage. And once there is a stage, there is an audience.

Public posturing is not irrational. It serves a function. Leaders signal strength. Representatives reassure constituents. Executives try to calm shareholders. Elected officials protect political capital. The problem is not that public statements exist. The problem is when negotiators forget that public language and private problem-solving operate under different rules.

If you don't understand this distinction, you will negotiate with the speech instead of the situation.

The Principle

Public statements protect identity, not just position.

When someone takes a hard line in public, they are rarely just arguing about substance. They are protecting identity, credibility, and perceived strength.

A labor leader who declares, "We will not accept a single concession," may privately understand that some trade-offs are inevitable. But publicly, their role requires strength. A CEO who announces, "We will not overpay," may privately recognize flexibility. But investors expect discipline.

Public posturing is often about signaling resolve to an audience rather than closing off options at the table.

Seasoned negotiators understand that public rigidity often masks private flexibility. They do not panic at bold statements. They listen for the underlying interests behind the amplified language.

They also understand a second truth: once someone has gone public, backing down becomes psychologically and politically expensive. The negotiation is no longer just about outcomes; it is about saving face. Your job is not to defeat the statement. Your job is to create a path where movement does not look like surrender.

The Pitfall

Escalating against the microphone.

The most common mistake is responding publicly to public posturing.

When one side issues a strong statement, the other side feels pressure to match it. The tone hardens. Language sharpens. Each press release becomes more absolute than the last. Soon the real negotiation is not happening at the table, it is happening in headlines, inboxes, and comment threads.

This is escalation by performance.

The deeper danger is psychological entrapment. The more extreme your public language becomes, the fewer off-ramps remain. Constituents expect you to “hold the line.” Any adjustment appears weak. What began as positioning becomes prison.

There is also a relational cost. Public rebuttals can humiliate the other side. And humiliation breeds retaliation, not cooperation.

In construction disputes, labor negotiations, corporate mergers, or community conflicts, the same dynamic appears: once leaders argue through the press or broad internal communications, trust erodes quickly. Private candor disappears. Every conversation is filtered through fear of exposure. The seasoned negotiator avoids negotiating through the microphone.

The Pointer

Separate the stage from the table.

When public posturing appears, take three deliberate steps.

First, do not overreact to the statement. Ask yourself. Who is the audience? What pressure are they managing? What identity are they protecting? Treat the statement as data, not a declaration of war.

Second, shift meaningful movement back to private channels. Real progress rarely happens in front of an audience. Create space for quiet conversation. A simple line works: “I understand the message you needed to send publicly. Let’s talk about what flexibility might look like privately.” This acknowledges their reality without endorsing their position.

Third, help them reframe movement as consistency, not

retreat. If you want the other side to move, give them language that preserves credibility. Craft proposals that can be explained as strength, prudence, responsibility, or responsiveness, not capitulation. For example, instead of forcing someone to "drop" a demand, help them say: "We've secured key protections and made strategic adjustments in the broader interest."

Movement becomes leadership, not weakness.

There is also a discipline required on your side: manage your own public messaging carefully. Avoid absolutes. Leave room to maneuver. Words like "never," "non-negotiable," and "final offer" feel powerful in the moment, but shrink your future options.

Experienced negotiators use calibrated language publicly and expansive thinking privately.

Public posturing often signals insecurity, not strength. When someone feels fully confident at the table, they rarely need dramatic public statements.

If you respond emotionally, you confirm the drama. If you respond strategically, you lower the temperature.

Remember: audiences are watching for strength, but strength does not require aggression. It requires steadiness. The negotiator who wins in public conflicts is not the loudest voice. It is the one who understands that two negotiations are happening simultaneously.

One for the audience and one for the outcome. Confuse them, and you harden positions. Separate them, and you create space for agreement. Public posturing is theater. Agreements are built backstage.

The disciplined negotiator knows when to let the curtain rise - and when to step behind it.

INSIGHT 39 – RESTORING WORKING RELATIONSHIPS AFTER A BLOWUP

Restoring a working relationship after a blowup is one of the most difficult moments a negotiator or leader faces. In the heat of conflict, words are said that were never meant to carry permanent weight, assumptions are made about motives, and trust can

fracture quickly. What was once a professional relationship built on cooperation can suddenly feel fragile, tense, and uncertain. Yet seasoned negotiators understand that the aftermath of a conflict is not simply about moving on, it is about deliberately repairing the conditions that allow people to work together again. The goal is not to pretend the conflict never happened, nor to force an immediate return to normal. Instead, it is to acknowledge what occurred, stabilize emotions, and reestablish enough mutual respect and clarity so progress becomes possible again.

Every long-term working relationship will eventually experience a rupture. A heated exchange in a project trailer. A sharp email copied to senior leadership. A public disagreement in front of a crew. The blowup itself is rarely the fatal event. What determines the future of the relationship is what happens next.

Strong professionals do not avoid conflict. They know how to repair it and restore working relationships after things have gone sideways.

The Principle

Repair is a leadership skill, not a personal favor.

Conflict rupture is not proof of failure. It is proof that pressure exists. Under deadline stress, cost overruns, safety incidents, or political tension, even capable people react poorly. The question is not whether someone "lost their cool." The question is whether the relationship can return to functional trust.

Restoration begins with recognizing that repair is a strategic act.

When a blowup occurs, three things are usually damaged:

1. Respect - Someone feels dismissed, embarrassed, or attacked.
2. Safety - Someone feels exposed or uncertain about future interactions.
3. Clarity - The issue itself becomes tangled with emotion.

Repair means intentionally separating the relationship from the incident. It means signaling that the working relationship still matters. Notice that this does not require agreement. It requires acknowledgment.

A strong repair conversation often includes four moves:

- Name the event without dramatizing it.
- Own your part without over-defending.
- Acknowledge impact without arguing intent.
- Refocus forward toward shared work.

For example: "Yesterday's meeting escalated. I contributed to that. That wasn't productive. We have too much important work ahead to let that sit between us." This does not assign total blame. It does not surrender substance. It restores the relational frame.

The seasoned negotiator understands that a unresolved

rupture quietly poisons every future conversation. Repair is not emotional housekeeping; it is operational necessity.

The Pitfall

Re-litigating the blowup.

The most common mistake after a rupture is attempting to “clear the air” by re-arguing the original issue. The repair meeting becomes round two. Instead of restoring stability, both sides rehearse grievances:

- “You started it.”
- “You misunderstood.”
- “That’s not what I meant.”
- “You always...”

Now the relationship absorbs a second hit.

Another common pitfall is the non-apology apology:

- “I’m sorry you felt that way.”
- “If you were offended...”

These statements minimize impact and protect ego. They communicate that the problem was perception, not behavior.

Equally damaging is avoidance. Professionals sometimes pretend nothing happened. They keep it “business only.” Outwardly, work continues. Internally, trust erodes. Communication becomes guarded. Emails get copied wider. Small disagreements escalate faster because the relational bank account is depleted.

Un-repaired conflict increases fragility. People interpret neutral actions negatively. Tone gets misread. Assumptions harden. The longer repair is delayed, the more narrative builds in the absence of conversation. Silence does not heal rupture. It calcifies it.

The Pointer

Separate the issue from the relationship.

The practical path forward is disciplined and simple.

Step 1: Go private. Repair should almost always happen one-on-one. Public reconciliation feels performative. Private repair feels genuine.

Step 2: Lower intensity before content. Do not begin with, "Let's revisit the numbers." Begin with, "I don't want yesterday to define how we work together."

Step 3: Take partial ownership. You are not accepting total blame. You are accepting your contribution. "I was sharper than I needed to be." "I let the pressure get the better of me." Ownership reduces defensiveness immediately.

Step 4: Acknowledge impact. Impact matters more than intent. "I imagine that came across as dismissive; I can see how that might have put you on the spot." You are not conceding the argument. You are validating the experience.

Step 5: Re-anchor to shared purpose. Repair gains strength when it ties back to mutual goals. "We both want this project to succeed." "We're on the same team here." Shared purpose re-establishes alignment without erasing differences.

Step 6: Then, and only then, address substance. Once the temperature drops, you can revisit the issue with more clarity and less ego. Sometimes full agreement will not emerge. That is acceptable. The goal of repair is not harmony. It is functionality.

In high-stakes environments, relationships outlast arguments. You may negotiate dozens of issues over years with the same counterpart. A single explosive moment does not have to define that arc. The professionals who rise over time are not the ones who never rupture. They are the ones who repair quickly, cleanly, and without theatrics.

Repair communicates maturity. Repair builds credibility. Repair increases influence.

When someone knows you can disagree fiercely and still restore respect, they trust you more, not less. Conflict tests a relationship. Repair strengthens it.

CHAPTER FIVE

STRATEGIC PREPARATION AND PROCESS CONTROL

"Sometimes the fastest way to resolution is not a better argument. It is a better setting. Choose your arena wisely."

INSIGHT 40 – PREPARATION BEYOND THE NUMBERS

Most negotiators believe preparation means mastering the numbers. They review budgets, calculate margins, analyze pricing models, and forecast possible concessions. While those elements matter, experienced negotiators know that numbers alone rarely

determine the outcome. Negotiations are shaped by people, by their pressures, fears, incentives, reputations, and the audiences they must answer to after the meeting ends. If preparation stops at spreadsheets and talking points, a negotiator walks into the room understanding the math but missing the dynamics that will actually drive the decision.

Preparation beyond the numbers means understanding the environment in which the negotiation lives. Skilled negotiators prepare for these realities the same way they prepare for pricing or contract terms.

If they walk into the room and get blindsided, it's usually by people and not by math. It happens because someone underestimated emotion, identity, politics, fear, ego, or internal pressure. Preparation beyond the numbers is what separates technicians from strategists.

The Principle

Prepare for the human system, not just the deal.

Numbers matter. Costs matter. Timelines matter.

But every negotiation lives inside a human system - full of competing interests, status dynamics, hidden vetoes, and reputational risks. If you prepare only your spreadsheet, you are preparing for a machine. If you prepare for the people, you are preparing for reality.

Beyond financial analysis, strategic preparation requires asking:

- Who feels exposed in this decision?
- Who benefits politically?
- Who loses status if this moves forward?
- Who can quietly block this later?
- What pressure are they under from above or below?
- What story do they need to tell internally after agreeing?

On a job-site, you may believe the issue is a $180,000 change order. But for the project executive, it may be about protecting quarterly margins. For the superintendent, it may be about not looking incompetent. For the owner's rep, it may be about avoiding scrutiny from their board. The numbers are the visible layer. The real negotiation lives underneath.

Preparation beyond the numbers means mapping power, pressure, perception, and pride. It means understanding that people rarely resist proposals because of math, they resist because of meaning.

The Pitfall

Overconfidence in logic.

The most common mistake professionals make is assuming that if their numbers are correct, their argument will win. They rehearse data. They refine calculations. They build airtight justifications. And then they present it like a courtroom closing statement.

When the other side hesitates, pushes back, or stalls, they double down. More data. More proof. More "rational" explanation. But resistance is often not about facts. It's about:

- Fear of setting precedent.
- Internal politics.
- Budget cycles.
- Saving face.
- Past resentment.
- Mistrust.

When someone says, "This seems high," they may mean, "If I approve this, I'll get hammered internally." When someone says, "We don't have the budget," they may mean, "I don't have the authority." When someone says, "We'll get back to you," they may mean, "I need to check with someone who can veto this."

If you prepared only numbers, you will hear objections as technical problems. If you prepared beyond the numbers, you will hear them as signals. Overconfidence in logic creates tunnel vision. It makes you argue harder when you should be diagnosing deeper. And nothing escalates a negotiation faster than feeling unheard.

The Pointer

Run a Four-Layer Preparation Drill.

Before your next significant negotiation, go beyond spreadsheets.

Run this four-layer preparation drill.

1. Financial Layer
   - Do the math.
   - Know your walk-away.
   - Understand your leverage.
   - Clarify what is non-negotiable.
2. Structural Layer
   - Who actually decides?
   - Who influences quietly?
   - Who could derail this after the meeting?
   - Is the decision made in the room—or elsewhere?
   - Never confuse attendance with authority.
3. Emotional Layer
   - What identity risks are involved?
   - Who might feel blamed?
   - Who might feel cornered?
   - Where might pride be fragile?
4. Narrative Layer - What story does each party need to tell afterward?
   - "We protected margin."
   - "We upheld standards."
   - "We were fair."
   - "We maintained control."
   - "We didn't get pushed around."

If your proposal makes the other side look weak internally, it will stall even if the numbers are sound. Preparation beyond the numbers includes crafting a solution that works technically and narratively.

Most professionals prepare to win arguments. Seasoned negotiators prepare to remove obstacles before they surface. They anticipate objections rooted in pride. They design proposals that preserve face. They sequence conversations so decision-makers are not surprised. They align allies before the formal meeting. They understand that timing is leverage and they watch for the hidden veto.

When they walk into the room, they are not surprised by resistance because they've already mapped it.

Preparation beyond the numbers is not soft. It is not abstract. It is strategic risk management. It recognizes that deals are made by humans operating inside systems of power and pressure.

If you only prepare the math, you prepare for ideal conditions. If you prepare for people, politics, and perception, you prepare for reality. And reality is where negotiations are actually won.

INSIGHT 41 – ISSUE STACKING AND SEQUENCING

Negotiations rarely collapse because of a single issue. They collapse because of how issues are handled. Skilled negotiators understand that progress is not just about what gets discussed, but when and in what order.

Issue stacking and sequencing is the discipline of structuring the negotiation so momentum builds rather than stalls. When done well, it creates psychological progress, preserves leverage, and opens pathways for trade-offs. When done poorly, it hardens positions and locks parties into corners.

The Principle

Structure Drives Outcome.

Negotiation is not a random exchange of demands; it is a designed sequence of decisions. Issue stacking means deliberately bundling multiple issues together so they can be traded. Sequencing means intentionally choosing the order in which those issues are discussed and resolved.

The main principle is concessions are more powerful when connected than when isolated. When issues are discussed one at a time and settled immediately, negotiators reduce flexibility. Every issue becomes a win-lose contest. The conversation becomes narrow and defensive. But when multiple issues are "on the table" at once, negotiators can make trades that expand value. For example:

- Price
- Schedule
- Scope
- Payment terms
- Risk allocation

If price is discussed alone, the only movement possible is up or down. But if price is connected to schedule flexibility, scope adjustments, or risk sharing, suddenly there are options.

Sequencing matters just as much as stacking. The order of discussion shapes tone and expectations. Early agreements on smaller or less controversial issues build momentum and signal good faith. Tackling the hardest issue first may appear bold, but it can also trigger defensiveness before trust has formed.

Conversely, postponing the most difficult issue too long can create a last-minute impasse that unravels everything. The seasoned negotiator understands three sequencing truths:

1. Early wins build psychological commitment.
2. Mid-negotiation trades create value.
3. The final issue often carries emotional weight disproportionate to its economic value.

Structure is not manipulation. It is strategy. You are not changing the substance of the negotiation; you are shaping the pathway through it.

The Pitfall

Accidental Concessions and Dead-End Discussions.

The most common mistake negotiators make is treating issues sequentially by default - and resolving them one at a time. It sounds efficient, “Let’s settle price first,” or “Now let’s move to delivery.” What feels orderly often becomes restrictive. When you settle price first without linking it to other variables, you give away your strongest bargaining chip. You lose the ability to say, “If we can adjust schedule, I may have flexibility on price.” You are left defending every remaining issue individually.

Another pitfall is failing to control sequencing when the other party pushes to isolate a single issue, usually the one most favorable to them.

For example, a counterpart may insist: “We need to finalize the price before we talk about anything else.” If you comply, you shrink the negotiation into a narrow tunnel.

A second sequencing mistake is tackling emotionally charged issues too early. When parties lead with grievances, accusations, or historical disputes, the negotiation begins under threat conditions. Cognitive bandwidth narrows and flexibility declines.

The opposite mistake also occurs - presenting the hardest issue last without preparing the ground. When all other issues are resolved and one remains, it becomes a symbolic battleground. Neither side wants to appear weak at the finish line. The result? Deadlock over something that might have been manageable earlier in the process.

Finally, poor stacking leads to unintentional concession patterns. When concessions are made piecemeal and unlinked, the other side learns a dangerous lesson: pressure produces movement.

Without intentional stacking, you train the other party to keep pushing.

The Pointer

Design the agenda before the argument.

Before you negotiate substance, negotiate structure. Ask yourself:

- What are all the issues in play?
- Which ones are high value to me but low cost to them?
- Which ones are low value to me but high value to them?
- Which issue is emotionally charged?
- Which issue is symbolic?

Write them all down then design the sequence. A practical sequencing framework looks like this:

1. Open with alignment issues. Start with areas of shared interest or low controversy. Build rhythm. Establish problem-solving tone.
2. Introduce mid-tier issues next. These are issues with moderate importance but trade potential. Begin bundling. Use conditional language: "If we can do X, could you consider Y?"
3. Stack before settling. Resist finalizing early agreements immediately. Keep issues tentatively open so they can be traded across if needed. Use

phrases like: "Let's mark that as provisional while we look at the bigger picture."

4. Tackle high-intensity issues with context. By the time you address the most difficult topic, you should have momentum, partial agreements, and relational stability. The negotiation now has ballast.
5. Close with a bundle. Package agreements together. This reinforces the idea of exchange rather than concession.

The language of stacking matters. Avoid: "I'll give you that." Instead use: "If we can align on schedule flexibility, I can move on price." Every concession should be conditional and connected.

Another powerful pointer is to make multi-issue proposals. Instead of offering movement on one item, present a package: "We could adjust scope slightly, hold price steady, and extend timeline by two weeks." Packages signal seriousness and strategic thinking. They also force the other side to evaluate the proposal as a whole rather than cherry-picking elements.

Finally, remember this, momentum is a psychological asset. People are more likely to agree when they feel progress. They are less likely to derail a deal when multiple agreements are already in place. Issue stacking and sequencing create that momentum intentionally.

Negotiation is rarely won through a single brilliant argument. It is won through disciplined structure. When you control how issues are grouped and when they are addressed, you shape the terrain of the negotiation. Stack issues to create trades. Sequence discussions to build momentum. Connect concessions so movement is mutual.

The negotiator who masters structure does not chase agreement, he designs it.

INSIGHT 42 – WHAT MUST BE DECIDED TOGETHER VS. SEPARATELY

Negotiations will sometime stall not because people disagree on substance, but because they disagree on process. One side wants to bundle everything. The other wants to separate issues. One insists, "We need to settle this as a package." The other replies,

"Let's handle one thing at a time."

What must be decided together and what should be decided separately is not a logistical detail. It is a strategic choice. And when handled poorly, it quietly shapes who wins, who loses, and whether trust survives.

The Principle

Sequence shapes outcomes.

The structure of decisions influences the substance of decisions. When issues are bundled together, trade-offs become possible. Concessions in one area can be exchanged for gains in another. Creativity expands. Value can be created because parties can prioritize differently.

When issues are separated, clarity increases. Each topic can be analyzed on its own merits. Emotional spillover is reduced and accountability sharpens.

Neither approach is inherently superior. The question is strategic:

- Are the issues interdependent?
- Does movement in one area unlock flexibility in another?
- Or does bundling create confusion, overwhelm, or coerce?

Experienced negotiators understand that decision structure is leverage. If salary, benefits, and job title are negotiated together, flexibility increases. If they are negotiated separately and sequentially, anchoring effects and commitment bias can lock in outcomes early.

Bundling expands possibility. Separating reduces noise. The key is alignment between issue design and decision dynamics. If issues are tightly connected, scope, price, and timeline, separating them artificially may produce distorted commitments. If issues are emotionally charged, bundling them may escalate tension.

The seasoned negotiator asks, does deciding this together increase clarity and joint gain? Or does it create pressure and distortion? Structure is strategy.

The Pitfall

Using Structure as a Weapon.

Where structure becomes dangerous is when it is used manipulatively. One common tactic is forced bundling. A party says, "This is the deal. Take it or leave it." Multiple issues are packaged in a way that makes it difficult to isolate fairness or evaluate components. The bundle hides imbalance.

Another common tactic is strategic fragmentation. A party insists on settling one issue at a time, knowing that early concessions weaken the other side's leverage for later issues. For example:

- First settle price.
- Then discuss scope.
- Then address change orders.

By the time scope expands, price is locked. By the time timeline shifts, commitments have hardened. Sequential decision-making can create a ratchet effect. The pitfall is not bundling or separating. The pitfall is failing to recognize when structure is distorting fairness or suppressing voices.

There is also a psychological trap. When emotions are high, parties often try to resolve everything at once. "Let's just clear the air." But combining past grievances, future commitments, financial terms, and relational repair in one conversation can overwhelm cognitive bandwidth. Too much at once produces defensiveness. Too little at once produces fragmentation. Poor sequencing creates accidental escalation.

Another pitfall is ignoring decision rights. Some issues must be decided together because they affect shared systems, budgets, safety standards, and resource allocations. Other issues are autonomous and should not require joint approval. Confusion about authority leads to unnecessary conflict. When everything is treated as joint, autonomy erodes. When nothing is treated as joint, alignment erodes. The failure to distinguish between shared decisions and independent decisions creates friction disguised as disagreement.

The Pointer

Diagnose interdependence before you decide.

Before debating substance, negotiate structure. Ask explicitly:

- Which issues are linked?
- Which decisions depend on others?
- What must be aligned?
- What can be handled independently?

This conversation alone reduces misinterpretation. If issues are economically linked, bundle them. If they are emotionally volatile, sequence them. If one decision constrains another, decide the constraint first. If clarity is needed, isolate the issue.

Decide Together When:

- The outcome affects both parties' long-term interests.
- Trade-offs can create mutual gain.
- Implementation requires coordination.
- Fairness depends on proportional exchange. Decide Separately When:
- Issues are emotionally charged and require containment.
- Authority differs across topics.
- Information is incomplete and requires phased clarity.
- One decision should not bias another.

There is also power wisdom here. When leverage is uneven, bundling can protect the weaker party by allowing trade-offs. Conversely, separating issues can prevent stronger parties from hiding imbalance inside complexity.

Be transparent about sequencing. Say, "some of these issues are connected. I think we'll get better outcomes if we look at them together. Others might deserve their own discussion so we don't blur them. Can we map that out first?" This reframes structure as collaborative rather than strategic.

In high-stakes environments, sequencing is often the invisible battlefield. Whoever controls order influences momentum. Early agreements create psychological commitment. Late-stage issues become harder to reopen.

A seasoned negotiator is deliberate about first moves. They do not accidentally concede early on issues that affect leverage later. They protect optionality. They resist premature closure on isolated components that are structurally linked. They understand that the question is not simply, "What are we deciding?" It is also, "In what order?" and "In what groupings?"

Timing influences pressure. Grouping influences fairness.

Structure influences power.

Many negotiations fail not because people disagree irreconcilably, but because they structure decisions poorly. If you do not intentionally design how decisions are made, the structure will design the outcome for you.

What must be decided together and what must be decided separately is never just procedural. It is strategic architecture.

INSIGHT 43 – CHOOSING THE FORUM

Negotiation is not only about what gets discussed or how it gets discussed. It is also about where it gets discussed. The forum you choose - a formal meeting, a private sidebar, a mediation room, an email exchange, a job-site walk, an executive boardroom, an

arbitration hearing, or a public hearing will shape behavior, tone, and leverage.

Many negotiators focus entirely on arguments and ignore the architecture of the conversation itself. Seasoned negotiators understand that choosing the forum is often one of the most strategic moves available.

The Principle

The forum shapes the outcome.

The setting is not neutral. Every forum carries built-in incentives, pressures, and psychological signals. A private conversation invites candor. A formal boardroom meeting signals accountability. A public hearing amplifies posture. A mediated session encourages problem-solving. Arbitration narrows focus to rights and evidence. An Email slows emotion but can harden positions. The forum determines:

- Who feels powerful.
- Who feels exposed.
- Whether saving face is possible.
- Whether flexibility is safe.
- Whether collaboration or combat is rewarded.

Consider a construction dispute between a general contractor and a subcontractor. In a crowded project meeting, accusations about delays trigger defensiveness. Each side must protect their reputation in front of owners and inspectors. This forum encourages public positioning.

Move that same conversation to a quiet trailer after hours, and the tone changes. Without audience pressure, both sides can admit constraints and explore trade-offs.

The seasoned negotiator asks first, "What behavior will this setting encourage?"

If you want collaboration, choose a forum that reduces audience pressure. If you need accountability, choose a forum that formalizes commitment. If you want clarity on legal rights, choose a forum that narrows scope to standards and evidence.

You are not just selecting a room. You are selecting a behavioral environment.

The Pitfall

Fighting in the wrong arena.

The most common mistake is arguing in a forum that rewards the wrong behavior. Three predictable errors appear repeatedly:

1. Trying to Collaborate in a Public Arena

When stakes are visible and reputations are on display, people posture. They defend positions harder than they would in private. What could have been solved with nuance becomes theatrical. Public settings amplify ego and reduce flexibility.

2. Trying to Threaten in a Collaborative Setting

Sometimes a negotiator introduces aggressive legal threats during what was intended to be a problem-solving session. The forum signals cooperation, but the message signals escalation. Trust fractures instantly. Misalignment between tone and forum creates instability.

3. Escalating Too Quickly to Formal Processes

Arbitration, litigation, or executive escalation can shut down creative options prematurely. Once lawyers are involved or senior leaders are present, people defend institutional positions rather than explore interests. Formal forums narrow thinking.

When negotiators choose the wrong arena, they unknowingly strengthen resistance. They make it harder for the other side to say “yes” safely. A classic example is sending a strongly worded email copying senior leadership instead of requesting a private call. The issue shifts from substance to status. The copied recipients become the silent audience that stiffens everyone’s spine. The conflict grows, not because the issue was unsolvable, but because the forum rewarded rigidity.

The Pointer

Match the forum to the goal.

Before initiating a difficult conversation, pause and answer three questions:

1. What outcome am I trying to produce?
2. What behavior must the other party feel safe enough to demonstrate?
3. Which setting makes that behavior more likely?
    - If you need candor - choose privacy.
    - If you need accountability - choose structure.
    - If you need creativity - choose informality.
    - If you need precedent - choose formal adjudication.
    - If you need de-escalation - remove the audience.

Forum choice is also dynamic. You can sequence forums intentionally:

- Start privately to surface interests.
- Move to a structured joint meeting to formalize agreements.
- Escalate only if collaboration fails.

This sequencing preserves flexibility while protecting authority.

Another advanced move is reframing the forum midstream. If a meeting turns theatrical, you can say, "This feels like it would benefit from a smaller conversation. Can we step aside and reset?" That single sentence changes the arena—and often the tone. Remember: you are not trapped by the initial setting. You can redesign the forum.

Some of the most productive negotiations happen outside formal rooms, walking a jobsite together, grabbing coffee, or reviewing drawings side-by-side. These settings reduce adversarial framing. They orient both parties toward a shared object (the project, the document, the task) rather than toward each other as opponents.

Physical orientation influences psychological orientation. Sitting across a table can feel oppositional. Standing shoulder-to-shoulder reviewing a plan feels collaborative.

Seasoned negotiators pay attention to physical geometry, audience size, hierarchy visibility, and timing. They understand that the room speaks before they do.

When conflict intensifies, most people escalate content. They argue harder. They collect more evidence. They sharpen their language. The strategic negotiator does something different. They pause and ask, "Is this the right forum?" Sometimes the fastest way to resolution is not a better argument. It is a better setting.

Choosing the forum is about understanding that negotiation is environmental. Context shapes courage. Audience shapes posture. Structure shapes flexibility.

This Principle reminds us that the forum influences behavior. The Pitfall warns against fighting in arenas that reward rigidity. The Pointer encourages deliberate alignment between setting and strategic goal.

Before your next difficult conversation, don't just prepare your talking points. Choose your arena wisely.

INSIGHT 44 – TIMING AS STRATEGY

Most negotiators obsess over what to say and how to say it. Far fewer think deeply about when to say it. Yet timing is not a cosmetic detail in negotiation, it also is structural. The same proposal offered at two different moments can land as either an insult or a breakthrough. The same silence can read as weakness or strength depending on when it is used.

Timing is not patience alone. It is not delay for delay's sake. Timing is the strategic use of sequence, momentum, pressure, and readiness.

If you ignore timing, you fight uphill. If you master timing, the slope works for you.

The Principle

Timing shapes perception and leverage.

In negotiation, value is not static. Urgency rises and falls. Attention sharpens and dulls. Risk tolerance expands and contracts. Timing influences all of it.

A proposal made before the other side feels the problem will likely be dismissed. The same proposal made when the cost of inaction becomes clear may suddenly feel reasonable.

The principle is simple; people move when the pain of staying put exceeds the fear of change. Your job is not merely to craft good terms. It is to introduce those terms when the conditions make movement possible. Timing operates on several levels:

- Emotional timing - Is the other party regulated or reactive?
- Informational timing - Do they yet understand the implications?
- Organizational timing - Are decision-makers aligned?
- External timing - Are deadlines real, artificial, or flexible?
- Relational timing - Is trust sufficient for risk-taking?

Experienced negotiators read tempo the way a conductor reads a score. They know when to slow the room, when to let silence stretch, when to accelerate toward decision, and when to step back.

They understand that pushing too early triggers resistance. Waiting too long invites drift. Timing is not about controlling the clock. It is about aligning movement with readiness.

The Pitfall

Forcing momentum or waiting passively.

The most common mistake around timing falls into two extremes.

1. Premature Acceleration - Impatience is expensive.
    - You present numbers before interests are clear.
    - You demand agreement before trust exists.
    - You escalate before options are explored.

Premature acceleration often comes from anxiety, your own deadlines, pressure from your organization, or fear of losing leverage. But forcing a decision before the other side has psychologically crossed the bridge guarantees pushback. What feels like urgency to you feels like coercion to them. The result? Positions harden. Concessions shrink. Resentment grows. Remember, speed without readiness creates resistance.

2. Passive Waiting - The opposite mistake is equally costly: waiting for "the right time" without shaping it.
    - You delay difficult conversations.
    - You avoid raising uncomfortable truths.
    - You assume the other side will eventually realize what you see.

Time does not automatically improve leverage. Sometimes it erodes it. Deadlines pass. Budgets close. Leadership changes. Informal agreements calcify into expectations. Waiting without strategy is not patience, it is drift.

Passive negotiators confuse inaction with wisdom. But time rarely works for both sides equally. If you are not shaping the timing, someone else is.

The Pointer

Shape the clock — don't chase it.

Seasoned negotiators treat timing as something to influence, not endure. Here are four practical ways to do that.

1. Test Readiness Before Advancing. Before introducing a major proposal, probe for psychological readiness:
    - "What concerns would we need to address before this feels workable?"
    - "If we were to move forward this quarter, what would have to be true?"

These questions surface barriers before you trigger resistance. If readiness is low, build conditions first. If readiness is rising, move decisively.

2. Sequence Information Strategically. Timing is often about order.
    - Lead with shared facts before disputed interpretations.
    - Address interests before numbers.
    - Resolve process before substance.

When you jump straight to terms, you skip necessary emotional and cognitive steps. But when you layer the conversation deliberately, momentum builds organically. Good timing is often good sequencing.

3. Use Silence as a Temporal Tool. Silence stretches time.

After making a proposal, resist the urge to fill the space. Let the other side sit with it. Let the weight of decision register. Silence increases perceived gravity. It signals confidence. It allows the room to process.

But silence must be intentional. If you look anxious or apologetic, it reads as uncertainty. If you look grounded, it reads as strength. Time expands under silence. Use that expansion deliberately.

4. Distinguish Real Deadlines from Artificial Ones. Not all deadlines are equal.

Some are externally fixed, regulatory filings, funding expirations, construction mobilizations, and fiscal year closures. Others are negotiation tactics.

Experienced negotiators test urgency:

- "What happens if we miss that date?"
- "Is there flexibility in the sequence?"
- "Who is impacted if this were to shift?"

When a deadline is real, respect it. When it is artificial, don't let it rush you into poor decisions. Timing as strategy requires clarity about which clocks actually matter.

There is another dimension rarely discussed. Sometimes the right move is not to press your advantage when you can – but to wait until the relationship can absorb the pressure. You may have leverage, you may have information and you may have the upper hand. But if the other side feels cornered too publicly or too abruptly, they will fight, not because your proposal is unreasonable, but because their identity feels threatened.

The seasoned negotiator asks, "Is now the moment that preserves both movement and dignity?" Timing is not only about outcomes. It is about sustainability.

My experience tells me that negotiation is not just an exchange of terms. It is a rhythm. Push too early and you create resistance. Wait too long and you lose momentum. Move with awareness and you create flow. Timing is strategy because it shapes perception, readiness, and leverage. The goal is not speed. The goal is alignment. When you introduce the right idea at the right moment, when urgency meets clarity and trust meets pressure, agreements do not feel forced. They feel inevitable.

INSIGHT 45 – CONTROLLING THE AGENDA

In negotiation, whoever controls the agenda often controls the outcome. Not because they dominate the room, but because they shape what gets attention, in what order, and under what assumptions. Most negotiators focus on arguments. Skilled

negotiators focus on structure and the agenda is structure.

When you control the agenda, you influence what problems are defined, what standards are considered legitimate, what options are explored, and what decisions feel urgent. You determine whether the conversation is reactive or deliberate. Whether it is tactical or strategic. Agenda control is not about manipulation. It is about intentional design.

The Principle

Structure drives substance.

The principle of agenda control is simple: what gets discussed and in what sequence, shapes what gets decided. An agenda is not a list of topics. It is decision planning. If price is discussed first, everything else becomes a concession around price. If scope is clarified first, price becomes a function of value. If grievances are aired first, trust erodes before solutions are even attempted. If shared goals are defined first, tension lowers before difficult trade-offs begin.

Agenda order frames perception. Skilled negotiators understand that discussions are path-dependent. Early framing influences later thinking. Psychologists call this anchoring; negotiators experience it as momentum. Once a conversation starts down a particular track, it becomes increasingly difficult to reverse direction.

Agenda control also determines emotional climate. Opening with accusations escalates defensiveness. Opening with shared objectives stabilizes identity. Opening with constraints clarifies reality. Each starting point creates a different psychological environment.

Agenda design answers three critical questions:

1. What must be clarified before value can be created?
2. What issues are emotionally volatile and require containment?
3. What sequence will build momentum rather than resistance? Strong negotiators do not "wing it." They propose structure early.
   - "Before we talk numbers, can we align on scope?"
   - "Let's outline the issues first so we don't miss anything."
   - "Would it make sense to separate short-term fixes

from long-term solutions?"

Notice the language. It is collaborative, not controlling. Agenda leadership is most effective when it feels like facilitation rather than dominance. When done well, the other side experiences clarity, not coercion. Structure reduces chaos. And clarity builds confidence.

The Pitfall

Confusing control with domination.

The most common mistake in agenda control is confusing structure with force. Some negotiators attempt to control the agenda by bulldozing:

- "We're not discussing that."
- "That's irrelevant."
- "Here's what we're going to cover."

This triggers resistance immediately. When people feel silenced, they push harder. When they feel ignored, they escalate. Attempts to rigidly impose structure often create the very disorder they were meant to prevent.

Another mistake is surrendering the agenda entirely. Many negotiators walk into meetings with no defined sequence. They respond to whatever issue is raised first. They allow the loudest voice to determine direction. They chase objections instead of guiding conversation. This creates reactive negotiation. And reactive negotiation usually favors the party with stronger emotional intensity, greater preparation, or positional leverage.

There is also a more subtle pitfall, hiding controversial items at the end. Some negotiators stack easy topics first and quietly leave difficult issues for "later," hoping time pressure will force compromise. While sequencing matters, strategic avoidance damages trust. When the other side realizes something was withheld or delayed intentionally, credibility erodes.

Agenda control should increase transparency, not manipulate timing to trap the other side.

Finally, overloading the agenda is a hidden trap. When too many issues are introduced simultaneously, cognitive overload sets in. Clarity decreases. Emotional regulation drops. People revert to positional thinking. Effective agenda control simplifies rather than complicates.

If you cannot summarize the structure of your negotiation in three to five categories, you probably have not clarified it enough.

The Pointer

Design the conversation before you enter it.

The practical pointer is draft the agenda before the meeting and propose it early. Preparation should include a written structure, even if informal. Identify:

- Primary objectives.
- Secondary trade-offs.
- Sensitive topics.
- Required decision points.
- Desired sequencing.

Ask yourself: What must be agreed upon before anything else makes sense?

Then test your structure against three filters:

1. Clarity Filter - does the sequence reduce confusion?
2. Momentum Filter - does it create small early agreements before larger ones?
3. Stability Filter - does it manage emotional risk before introducing volatility?

When the meeting begins, suggest the structure calmly, “I drafted a quick outline to help us stay focused. We can adjust it together if needed." This phrase accomplishes three things:

- It signals preparation.
- It invites collaboration.
- It positions you as process leader without appearing authoritarian.

If the other side proposes a different structure, resist reflexive rejection. Instead ask:

- "What outcome are you hoping that order achieves?"
- "What feels most urgent to you?"
- "Would it help if we separated those two issues?"

Agenda control is flexible leadership, not rigid enforcement.

When discussions drift, and they will, return to structure gently:

- "How about we park that for a moment and come back to the sequence we agreed on."
- "That's important. Can we capture it and revisit after we finish this section?"

These small resets prevent derailment without creating friction. Also remember, agenda control is continuous. It is not a one-time act at the beginning. Skilled negotiators recalibrate structure throughout the conversation. They notice when energy spikes. They notice when confusion increases. They notice when progress stalls. Then they adjust.

Sometimes control means accelerating, sometimes it means slowing down and sometimes it means breaking a large issue into smaller pieces. The agenda is not a document. It is a steering mechanism. Controlling the agenda does not guarantee agreement. But it dramatically increases the probability of intelligent dialogue.

Without structure, negotiation becomes emotional improvisation. With structure, negotiation becomes deliberate problem-solving. The side that controls the agenda does not control people. They control the path and the path determines where you land.

INSIGHT 46 – INFORMATION DISCIPLINE

In negotiation and leadership, information feels like oxygen. The instinct is to gather more of it, share more of it, and react quickly to it. But more information does not automatically mean better outcomes. In fact, unmanaged information can destabilize strategy,

fracture alignment, and erode leverage.

Information discipline is not secrecy. It is control. It is the intentional management of what you gather, what you share, when you share it, and how you interpret it. Without discipline, information controls you. With discipline, you control the process.

In competitive negotiations, parties typically have conflicting interests and limited alignment of incentives. Each side is attempting to achieve the most favorable outcome possible, often within a zero-sum framework where one side's gain is perceived as the other side's loss. Because of this structure, information becomes a form of leverage. The disciplined negotiator recognizes that every piece of information shared can alter the balance of power. Revealing deadlines, internal pressures, budget limits, or fallback positions can weaken negotiating strength. Once information is disclosed, it cannot be reclaimed. This does not mean negotiators should be deceptive or dishonest. Ethical negotiation requires accuracy.

Collaborative negotiation requires sharing the right information to enable joint problem solving, while still maintaining professionalism and clarity. One of the most frequent negotiation errors is using collaborative disclosure in competitive environments—or competitive secrecy in collaborative ones. Excessive secrecy in collaborative negotiations can produce distrust. When someone refuses to share relevant information that affects joint outcomes, the other side begins to assume hidden agendas.

The Principle

Information is leverage only when managed.

Information has power in three ways:

1. What you know.
2. What they know.
3. What each side believes the other knows.

The disciplined negotiator understands that raw information is neutral. It becomes leverage only when filtered, framed, and timed correctly. Most professionals assume transparency equals trust and silence equals manipulation. That assumption is naïve. Trust is built through consistency and clarity – not through oversharing. Strategic silence and thoughtful disclosure are not unethical; they are responsible stewardship of position.

Information discipline operates on three core rules:

1. Separate data from interpretation. Facts are neutral. Stories are not. "The schedule slipped two weeks" is data. "They are incompetent" is interpretation. The disciplined leader guards against confusing the two.
2. Share intentionally, not emotionally. Emotion-driven disclosure often reveals more than intended. Under pressure, people justify, defend, and explain excessively. The result is leakage of strategic information that was never required.
3. Release information in alignment with purpose. Timing matters. Early disclosure can strengthen credibility, or weaken leverage. Late disclosure can protect position, or damage trust. Discipline means aligning disclosure with objective, not anxiety.

In high-stakes situations, information discipline becomes the backbone of strategic clarity. It prevents overreaction to noise, protects alignment within your own team, and ensures that what is said advances your outcome.

The Pitfall

Information sprawl and emotional leakage.

The most common failure in negotiation is not misinformation. It is information sprawl. Information sprawl happens when:

- Too many people are speaking.
- Too much detail is shared without filtering.
- Internal disagreements become external signals.
- Updates are reactive rather than structured.

When teams lack discipline, three predictable problems arise.

First, internal misalignment leaks externally. Side conversations, contradictory emails, and offhand comments create uncertainty. The other side begins to sense fragmentation and presses harder.

Second, emotion overrides judgment. Under stress, people explain more than necessary. They reveal constraints. They disclose internal pressures. They admit bottom lines unintentionally. In trying to defend credibility, they sacrifice leverage.

Third, noise gets mistaken for signal. Every rumor feels urgent. Every complaint feels catastrophic. Leaders begin reacting to fragments of information instead of patterns. Strategy becomes reactive instead of deliberate.

In construction environments, for example, a single comment on the job-site – "We're behind because procurement messed up" can cascade into owner concern, subcontractor blame, and defensive documentation. What began as frustration becomes formal positioning.

The disciplined leader pauses before responding. They verify.

They filter. They ask: "Is this signal, or is this noise?"

Without discipline, information becomes an accelerant. With discipline, it becomes a stabilizer.

The Pointer

Build an information protocol before you need it.

Information discipline cannot be improvised in the heat of escalation. It must be designed in advance. Here are five practical moves to implement immediately:

1. Define a Single Voice - decide who speaks externally on key issues. Fragmented messaging destroys credibility. Even if multiple stakeholders are involved, external communication must be unified. This does not silence others. It channels them.
2. Establish a Filter Question - Before sharing anything, ask: Does this advance our objective?

Is this necessary for this audience? Is this the right time?

If the answer to any is no, pause.

3. Create Internal Containment - Encourage internal candor but external discipline. Teams must have a safe place to debate openly and privately. Once alignment is reached, the message going out must be cohesive. Internal disagreement is healthy. External contradiction is costly.
4. Slow Down Disclosure Under Pressure - Escalation compresses time. That is precisely when discipline matters most. When asked a difficult question, the disciplined negotiator does not rush to fill silence. They clarify, "Help me understand what specifically you're concerned about." This buys time. It gathers more information.

It prevents unnecessary revelation. Silence, when intentional, is information control.

5. Track Patterns, Not Episodes - one complaint does not

equal systemic failure. One delay does not equal collapse. Disciplined leaders look for trends before reacting. They avoid overcorrecting based on isolated data points.

Information is most dangerous when taken out of context. Information discipline is strategic calm. Information discipline is emotional discipline expressed through communication. It requires resisting three temptations:

- The temptation to prove.
- The temptation to defend.
- The temptation to vent.

Every unnecessary explanation reduces mystery. Every reactive disclosure reduces leverage. Every careless comment expands risk.

The seasoned negotiator understands that credibility is built not by constant talking, but by consistent positioning. They are transparent about process, measured about constraints, and deliberate about commitments.

They do not hide information. They steward it. They understand that power often lies not in what is said, but in what is withheld until the right moment. Information discipline creates three strategic advantages:

- Clarity – internally aligned messaging.
- Credibility – consistent external communication.
- Control – measured timing of disclosure.

In complex negotiations, the side that manages information best often shapes the narrative. And the side that shapes the narrative often shapes the outcome. The question is not whether information will flow. It always does. The question is whether it flows through you or around you. Information discipline ensures it flows through you. That is not secrecy. That is strategy.

INSIGHT 47 – CONCESSIONS WITH INTENTIONS

In every negotiation, concessions are inevitable. No agreement is reached without movement. Yet movement alone does not create progress. Too often, concessions are made reactively, offered to reduce tension, fill silence, or signal goodwill. The result? Value leaks

away, leverage erodes, and the final agreement feels unbalanced.

Concessions are not giveaways. They are instruments. And like any instrument, they must be played with intention.

Disciplined negotiators treat concessions as strategic moves rather than emotional reactions. Used intentionally, they build momentum, reinforce credibility and move both sides toward a workable agreement. Used poorly, they eat away at leverage and reset the negotiation in the other side's favor.

The Principle

Every concession must advance a purpose.

A concession should accomplish something measurable. It should reduce uncertainty, build reciprocity, clarify commitment, narrow the zone of agreement, or move the other party closer to a decision. If it does none of these, it is not a concession, it is a surrender. Concessions are signals and they communicate three things:

1. Flexibility - You are capable of movement.
2. Limits - You are not infinitely flexible.
3. Expectation of Reciprocity - Movement invites movement.

When you give something without tying it to purpose, you dilute all three signals.

Skilled negotiators think in terms of exchanges, not sacrifices. They rarely say, "We can lower the price." Instead, they say, "If we can agree on the timeline, we can revisit the price." The concession is conditional. It is structured. It is attached to progress.

Intentional concessions also follow a pattern: they tend to get smaller over time. Large early concessions communicate desperation. Gradually decreasing concessions communicate nearing limits. This psychological signal shapes the other party's expectations and protects your final position.

Intentional concessions are never impulsive. They are prepared in advance. Before negotiations begin, seasoned negotiators identify:

- What they can concede easily.
- What is costly to concede.
- What appears valuable to the other side but costs little to them.

- What they must never concede.

Preparation transforms concessions from reactive gestures into strategic tools.

The key insight: a concession is not about what you give. It is about what you gain in exchange.

The Pitfall

Conceding to relieve discomfort.

Most concession mistakes are emotional, not tactical. Silence stretches. The other party resists. Tension rises. Someone feels the need to "keep things moving." So, they offer a concession, often prematurely.

This is the most common and expensive mistake in negotiation: conceding to relieve pressure rather than to create progress. Pressure can take many forms:

- Awkward silence.
- Frustration or irritation.
- Aggressive demands.
- Implied urgency.
- Fear of losing the deal.

Under pressure, people equate movement with momentum. But movement without direction is drift. Another common pitfall is unconditional concessions. When you give without asking for something in return, you teach the other party a lesson, concessions come free. And human nature being what it is, they will test for more.

There is also the trap of "nibbling." You reach agreement, and at the end the other side asks for just one small additional item. It seems minor. You agree. But that small concession sends a message that your boundaries are flexible even at the finish line.

Over time, patterns of reactive concessions damage

credibility. If your first offer is followed quickly by meaningful movement, the other side learns your opening position was inflated. Future negotiations begin with skepticism.

Finally, emotional concessions often create internal resentment. You may secure a deal, but feel you "gave too much." That dissatisfaction shows up later, in reduced commitment, strained relationships, or unwillingness to collaborate. Concessions made without intention solve the discomfort of the moment while creating strategic problems later.

The Pointer

Make concessions conditional, gradual, and visible.

Disciplined negotiators follow three practical rules.

1. Always Attach a Condition. Never give something for nothing. Even if the return seems small, link your concession to a reciprocal move.

Instead of: "We can extend the deadline." Try: "If we extend the deadline, can we agree to finalize the scope today?" This accomplishes three things:

- It frames the concession as valuable.
- It reinforces reciprocity.
- It advances the negotiation toward closure.

Conditions do not have to be equal in value. They have to reinforce the exchange principle.

2. Concede in Decreasing Increments. Your concession pattern tells a story. Large early concessions followed by small ones communicate nearing limits. Large concessions throughout communicate weakness.

Think of concessions as steps down a staircase. Each step should be smaller than the last. This signals that you are approaching your boundary. It also encourages the other side to move more aggressively if they want agreement before the staircase ends.

The rhythm of concessions shapes perception more than absolute numbers.

3. Make Concessions Visible. If you concede quietly, the other side may not recognize the movement. Explicitly acknowledge it. "We're moving from 60 days to 45 days - that's meaningful flexibility on our end."

Visibility reinforces value. It prevents normalization. It ensures your movement is seen as deliberate, not automatic. You can also strategically pause before conceding. A brief break communicates consideration and cost. Instant concessions communicate ease.

Intentional concessions require discipline and patience. They require comfort with silence. They require clarity about your priorities. Before you concede, ask yourself three questions:

1. What does this move accomplish?
2. What am I receiving in return?
3. What precedent does this set for the rest of the negotiation?

If you cannot answer those clearly, wait. Concessions are not signs of weakness. They are signs of control when used properly. They demonstrate flexibility without surrender and collaboration without capitulation.

The most powerful negotiators are not those who refuse to move. They are those who move with precision. In the end, negotiation is not about how much you give. It is about how intentionally you give it.

Concede with purpose, concede with structure, and concede with expectation. When concessions have intentions, agreements gain strength and so do you.

INSIGHT 48 – CLOSING WITHOUT CREATING RESENTMENT

Deals do not fall apart at the beginning. They fracture at the end.

The final moments of a negotiation are emotionally charged. Fatigue sets in. Numbers tighten. Pride stiffens. People who have cooperated for hours suddenly shift into survival mode. The temptation is strong to "finish it" to squeeze, to press, to extract that last concession because you can feel the agreement within reach. And that is precisely where resentment is born.

A skilled negotiator understands that how you close determines whether the agreement lives in cooperation or dies in quiet retaliation.

The Principle

A sustainable close preserves dignity.

Every negotiation closes twice. First, it closes on paper. Second, it closes in the mind of the other party.

If the other side walks away feeling cornered, embarrassed, or diminished, the deal may be signed, but it will not be supported. Compliance will replace commitment. Energy will drop. Creativity will disappear and small problems will become big ones.

Closing without resentment means preserving the other party's sense of agency, competence, and respect. People can accept difficult terms. They cannot accept feeling small. A strong close does three things:

1. Affirms mutual progress. It highlights what has been accomplished together.
2. Frames concessions as reciprocal. It reinforces that movement happened on both sides.
3. Protects face. It allows the other party to explain the agreement positively to their stakeholders.

Resentment grows when someone feels they "lost." Satisfaction grows when someone feels they "chose." The difference lies in how the closing moment is handled. A sustainable close sounds like: "We've both stretched to get here. Let's make sure this works for both of us."

An extractive close sounds like: "If you really want this deal, you'll agree to this last point." Both may result in a signature but only one results in partnership.

The Pitfall

The victory lap close.

The most common mistake at the closing stage is overplaying leverage at the finish line.

After hours of back-and-forth, one-party senses advantage. Maybe deadlines are looming. Maybe alternatives are weaker. Maybe momentum favors them. And so, they push just a little more. "Since we're basically there, can you also include..." "One more adjustment and we're done." "This is the best you're going to get." It feels small. Tactical. Efficient. But to the other side, it feels like being trapped.

The psychological impact of a late-stage squeeze is disproportionate. By the time negotiators approach agreement, emotional energy is low and cognitive flexibility is reduced. A last-minute demand feels like betrayal especially if it violates the spirit of collaboration built earlier.

Even worse is the subtle victory lap: "We got everything we needed." "That worked out well for us." Statements like these may be factually true. They are strategically disastrous.

Humans are acutely sensitive to fairness. Research in behavioral economics repeatedly shows that people will reject objectively beneficial agreements if they perceive them as unfair. The emotional sting of imbalance outweighs rational gain. A deal that feels one-sided will be revisited later through slow-walking implementation, rigid interpretation, passive resistance, or aggressive renegotiation.

Resentment does not explode immediately. It accumulates interest.

Another closing mistake is rushing acknowledgment. Teams often focus so intently on final terms that they skip relational closure. No appreciation. No recognition of effort. No signal o respect. Silence where gratitude should be leaves a vacuum where resentment grows. Closing is not just a transactional act. It is relational punctuation.

The Pointer

Close in a way that builds forward momentum.

If you want an agreement that lasts, shift from extraction to alignment in the final phase. Here are five practical moves:

1. Signal the End Intentionally. Say it clearly: "It feels like we're close. Let's make sure we land this in a way that works long term." This reframes closing as mutual completion rather than unilateral victory.
2. Summarize Shared Wins. Before reviewing final terms, summarize progress: "We clarified scope, protected your timeline, and secured pricing stability. That's meaningful movement." This reinforces joint effort and shared accomplishment.
3. Trade, Don't Take. If something remains unresolved, avoid asking for unilateral concessions. Instead say: "If we can align on X, I can commit to Y." Movement at the end should always be reciprocal. Even symbolic reciprocity preserves dignity.
4. Offer Future Framing. Help the other side explain the agreement positively: "When you present this internally, you can emphasize the schedule protection and risk reduction." You are not manipulating. You are protecting their ability to stand behind the deal.
5. Close with Respect. End with acknowledgment: "I appreciate how directly you handled the tough parts. That made this productive." Respect at the end cements goodwill.

Ask yourself two questions:

- Would I feel good explaining this agreement to my team if I were on the other side?
- Does this close increase the likelihood of collaboration next time?

If the answer to either is no, you are extracting value at the expense of relationship equity. Short-term gain can cost long-term access.

In industries where parties see each other repeatedly, reputation compounds. People remember how they felt more than what they signed. The best negotiators understand that the closing moment is not the time to dominate. It is the time to stabilize.

They resist the urge to spike the ball. They make room for dignity. They leave the table in a way that invites the next conversation. Because a deal well closed is not one where you win. It is one where no one feels they lost.

CHAPTER SIX

COGNITIVE TRAPS AND PSYCHOLOGICAL REALITY

"People defend who they are before they defend what they want. Affirm identity and stabilize the conflict."

Insight 49. Confirmation Bias

Insight 50. Attribution Error

Insight 51. Loss Aversion on the Job-site

Insight 52. Reactive Devaluation

Insight 53. Ego Investment

Insight 54. Overconfidence in Experience

Insight 55. The Pressure of Constituents

Insight 56. Identity-Based Conflict

Insight 57. Fear of Appearing Weak

Insight 58. The Discipline of Perspective

INSIGHT 49 – CONFIRMATION BIAS

Every negotiator believes they are objective. Every leader believes they are reasonable. Every project manager believes they are "just looking at the facts."

And yet, most conflicts are fueled not by a lack of information but by selective interpretation of it. Confirmation bias is the silent architect of misunderstanding. It doesn't shout. It nods. It quietly reinforces what you already think is true.

The danger is not that you have biases. The danger is that you don't notice them working.

The Principle

Your mind is a lawyer, not a judge.

Confirmation bias is the tendency to search for, interpret, and remember information in ways that confirm pre-existing beliefs. Once you form a conclusion, about a person, a subcontractor, a vendor, a client, or a negotiating counterpart, your mind begins building a case to support it.

It stops asking, “What else could be true?” It starts asking, “How do I prove I’m right?” In negotiation and conflict, this shift is subtle but decisive.

If you believe the other side is unreasonable, you will notice every rigid statement and ignore every flexible one. If you believe someone is incompetent, you will catalog their mistakes and overlook their competence. If you believe you are being treated unfairly, every ambiguous action will feel intentional. Your brain acts like a defense attorney for your existing narrative.

The seasoned negotiator understands this. The first story you tell yourself is rarely the most accurate one. They assume distortion is present - especially in high-pressure moments. They actively look for disconfirming evidence. They test their own conclusions and they don’t trust clarity that comes too quickly. They pause and ask:

- What facts contradict my current interpretation?
- What would someone neutral say about this situation?
- If I’m wrong, where would the evidence show up?

The principle is simple but uncomfortable: certainty is often a signal to slow down. When your position feels obviously correct, confirmation bias is usually already at work.

The Pitfall

Building a case instead of building a solution.

The most common mistake negotiators make under confirmation bias is turning the interaction into a courtroom. They begin gathering proof, they rehearse arguments, they curate selective examples and they repeat old grievances as validation. The conversation stops being about solving the problem and starts being about winning the narrative.

On a construction site, for example, a project manager may conclude that a subcontractor is "always late." From that moment forward, every delay becomes proof of irresponsibility, even when delays are weather-related or caused upstream. The subcontractor, sensing mistrust, becomes defensive. Productivity drops. Communication tightens. What began as a hypothesis becomes a self-fulfilling pattern.

Confirmation bias doesn't just distort perception. It alters behavior. And altered behavior produces the very outcomes you feared.

Another version of the pitfall appears in negotiation prep. A leader may assume the other side "won't move on price." As a result, they never explore creative structures, phased delivery, or scope trade-offs. They approach rigidly and receive rigidity in return.

The tragedy is this: confirmation bias narrows the solution space before the conversation even begins. It convinces you that the map is complete — when in reality, you've only drawn half of it. Worse, once publicly committed to your narrative, your ego attaches to it. Backtracking feels like weakness. Admitting new information feels like surrender.

So, you double down. The mind prefers consistency over accuracy. And negotiations collapse not because agreement was impossible, but because perception was never questioned.

The Pointer

Install structured doubt.

You cannot eliminate confirmation bias. But you can design around it. Seasoned negotiators don't rely on willpower. They use structure. Here are three practical safeguards:

1. Write the Opposing Argument Stronger Than They Would. Before a critical conversation, articulate the other side's case as convincingly as possible. Don't caricature it. Strengthen it. If you can't argue their position persuasively, you don't understand it yet. This exercise exposes blind spots and forces intellectual humility.
2. Separate Observation from Interpretation. Instead of saying, "They're trying to squeeze us," state observable facts: "They asked for a 7% reduction and referenced market pricing." Interpretation layers meaning onto facts. Bias lives in that layer. By separating the two, you slow emotional escalation and clarify what is actually known.
3. Invite Disconfirming Feedback. In team settings, assign someone the role of challenger. Ask: "What are we missing?" or "What would make our assumption wrong?" Encourage dissent before external conflict exposes it. Structured dissent prevents collective confirmation bias which is even more dangerous than individual bias.

On a job-site, this might mean asking foremen to flag schedule risks that contradict the optimistic master plan. In negotiation, it might mean stress-testing your BATNA assumptions before you present them. Structured doubt is not weakness. It is professional discipline.

Confirmation bias thrives in speed and certainty. It weakens under reflection and disciplined inquiry. The negotiator who masters this bias gains a quiet edge. They do not react to the first story. They do not defend every interpretation. They do not escalate based on assumption. Instead, they stay curious longer than others stay certain. And curiosity changes tone. It lowers defensiveness. It creates space for recalibration.

When someone feels misjudged, conflict hardens. When someone feels accurately understood, flexibility increases. Sometimes the most powerful move in negotiation is not a concession or a demand. It is the sentence: "Help me understand how you see this differently."

That question interrupts confirmation bias on both sides. It transforms adversaries into sources of data.

In the end, confirmation bias is not about intelligence. Highly intelligent people are often better at defending flawed conclusions. It is about the discipline to question your own narrative before challenging someone else's. The moment you assume you are seeing clearly...is often the moment you are not.

INSIGHT 50 – ATTRIBUTION ERROR

In negotiation and leadership, few cognitive traps are as persistent - or as costly - as attribution error. It is the reflex that leads us to explain other people's behavior as a function of their character while explaining our own behavior as a function of circumstance.

When they miss a deadline, they are irresponsible. When we miss a deadline, we were overloaded. When they push hard, they are greedy. When we push hard, we are protecting legitimate interests.

This distortion happens fast. It feels accurate. And it quietly erodes trust. Attribution error is not simply a psychological curiosity. It is a structural threat to good judgment.

The Principle

Behavior has more causes than character.

The central principle is simple: separate behavior from identity.

Most visible behavior in negotiation is situational before it is dispositional. Pressure, incentives, fear of internal backlash, performance metrics, budget constraints, ego threats, and misunderstood communication channels often drive what looks like personality.

The seasoned negotiator assumes complexity before assuming character.

When a subcontractor becomes defensive in a project meeting, the inexperienced manager thinks, "He's difficult." The experienced manager thinks, "Something just triggered pressure. What changed?"

When a supplier increases price without warning, the reflex may be, "They're taking advantage of us." A disciplined negotiator asks, "What market, cost, or internal constraint just shifted?"

This principle does not excuse bad behavior. It clarifies it. Attribution error narrows our lens. It converts a dynamic system into a moral judgment. And once behavior becomes a moral issue, resolution becomes a battle of righteousness rather than a problem-solving exercise.

The professional negotiator treats behavior as data first, character second.

The Pitfall

Escalating identity instead of addressing reality.

The danger of attribution error is escalation. When you attribute behavior to character, you respond to identity. And when people feel their identity attacked, they defend it. Consider a common pattern:

- Someone misses a deliverable.
- You interpret it as laziness or lack of commitment.
- Your tone sharpens.
- They sense accusation.
- They defend themselves.
- You interpret the defensiveness as proof of guilt.

Now both sides are negotiating about dignity instead of deadlines. This is how small operational issues turn into relational fractures.

The deeper pitfall is confirmation bias layered on top of attribution error. Once you label someone as "difficult," "unreasonable," or "untrustworthy," every future behavior is filtered through that story. Neutral actions feel hostile. Ambiguity feels intentional. Silence feels strategic.

And the more power you hold, the more dangerous this becomes. Leaders' attributions shape organizational narratives. If you casually describe a team as "weak" or a partner as "impossible," that framing spreads. It calcifies into culture.

Attribution error also blinds you to your own contribution. When you see the other party as the problem, you stop asking how your communication, timing, clarity, or tone may have influenced the situation. The result is predictable: hardened positions, reduced creativity, and stalled negotiations.

The Pointer

Replace judgment with curiosity.

The corrective is disciplined curiosity. Before labeling behavior, ask three questions:

1. What situational pressures might explain this? Deadlines? Internal politics? Cash flow? Reputation risk? Performance reviews?
2. What incentives are shaping their behavior? Are they rewarded for caution? For toughness? For cost containment? For visibility?
3. What might I be missing? Information gaps create stories. Stories often become character judgments.

A powerful practical tool is reframing statements internally. Instead of thinking, “They’re unreasonable,” shift to, “They are constrained by something I don’t yet understand.” That small linguistic change opens space.

Another tactic is to name the impact without naming character. Instead of: “You’re being uncooperative.” Try, “When the proposal changed without notice, it put our schedule at risk. Help me understand what shifted.”

Notice the difference. One attacks identity. The other invites explanation.

Seasoned negotiators also slow down their interpretation of tone. A raised voice may signal frustration. It may also signal stress, fatigue, or pressure from unseen stakeholders. Not every sharp response is personal. Not every hard demand is hostility.

Most importantly, examine your own side of the equation. Ask yourself:

- Did I provide clarity?
- Did I set realistic expectations?
- Did I create psychological safety?

- Did my tone escalate tension?

This is not self-blame. It is self-awareness. And self-awareness restores control. Attribution error thrives in speed. It weakens under reflection.

High-level negotiators protect relationships by managing attribution carefully. They avoid statements that globalize behavior.

- "You always..."
- "You never..."
- "This is who you are."

Global statements turn temporary behaviors into permanent labels. And permanent labels invite permanent resistance. Instead, they localize behavior:

- "In this instance..."
- "On this issue..."
- "In this situation..."

Localization keeps the door open. They also create structured debriefs after tense exchanges. Rather than privately concluding that the other party is difficult, they ask openly: "We seemed to hit friction earlier. Was that about the numbers, the timing, or something else?" This approach does something subtle but powerful: it gives the other side a way to attribute their own behavior to circumstance rather than defend character. When both sides move away from identity judgments, negotiation shifts from combat to coordination.

Attribution error is automatic. Correcting it is intentional. You will still feel the reflex to judge. That reflex is human. The discipline is not to eliminate it, but to pause before acting on it.

In negotiation, perception shapes response. Response shapes tone. Tone shapes trajectory. If you misdiagnose character when the real issue is context, you will apply the wrong remedy. And wrong remedies intensify problems.

The seasoned negotiator understands this: Most conflict is not about who someone is. It is about what someone is navigating.

When you replace judgment with curiosity, escalation with inquiry, and accusation with analysis, you reclaim strategic clarity. And, clarity is power.

INSIGHT 51 – LOSS AVERSION ON THE JOB-SITE

On a job-site, progress is visible. Steel rises. Concrete cures. Schedules advance. But so do costs, delays, and mistakes. And when something slips, time, money, or reputation, people react fast. Not because they are irrational, but because they are human.

Loss aversion is the invisible force behind many of the hardest conversations in construction. It explains why a superintendent fights harder over a back-charge than they negotiated over the original scope. Why an owner resists a change order more fiercely than they pursued value engineering. Why a subcontractor doubles down on a bad path rather than admit sunk costs.

The pain of losing feels stronger than the pleasure of gaining. On the job-site, that pain gets amplified by visibility, pride, and pressure.

It is critically important that you recognize loss aversion and manage it before it manages you.

The Principle

Losses loom larger than gains.

Behavioral economists Daniel Kahneman and Amos Tversky demonstrated that people experience losses roughly twice as intensely as equivalent gains. This is called loss aversion theory. In practical terms: losing $10,000 hurts more than gaining $10,000 feels good. On a job-site, losses aren't just financial. They are:

- Loss of face.
- Loss of authority.
- Loss of schedule.
- Loss of control.
- Loss of perceived competence.

When a framing crew falls behind, the superintendent may refer to the issue as "performance failure" rather than "sequence conflict," because acknowledging sequencing mistakes feels like a personal loss of credibility.

When an owner rejects a change order, they may not only be protecting the budget, they may be protecting the psychological commitment of "We are still on track."

Loss aversion also explains escalation. Once money, time, or reputation has been invested, people fight to avoid locking in the loss. They throw good resources after bad decisions because stopping would make the loss real.

In construction, stopping often feels like surrender. The seasoned negotiator understands this. Most resistance on the job-site is not about greed, it is about avoiding perceived loss. If you don't account for that, you misread the room.

The Pitfall

Triggering defensive behavior.

The biggest mistake leaders make on the job-site is unintentionally triggering loss reactions. You hear it in phrases like:

- "You're behind."
- "This is your fault."
- "We're charging you for this."
- "You missed it."

Each of these statements signals a loss. Of competence. Of money. Of status. Of control. When someone feels loss, they defend. They justify. They counterattack. They delay. They escalate.

Consider a real-world scenario. A concrete subcontractor underestimates labor on a pour. Overtime increases cost exposure. The GC points out productivity shortfalls in a coordination meeting, in front of peers. Objectively, the GC is correct. Psychologically, the subcontractor hears, "You failed publicly."

Now the subcontractor resists every subsequent coordination request. They scrutinize every RFI. They become rigid on scope interpretation. What changed? The schedule? No. What changed was perceived loss. Public correction created social loss. Financial pressure created economic loss. Pride amplified both. The result is not collaboration—it is entrenchment.

Another version happens with owners. If you present a change order as "additional cost due to your late design decision," the owner hears blame. Blame implies loss of competence and control. The conversation shifts from solving to defending.

Loss aversion also fuels sunk-cost bias. Crews continue

down inefficient paths because "we've already invested too much to change." Pulling back would make the prior investment feel wasted. So, they double down. The pitfall is assuming logic overrides emotion. It doesn't. Loss aversion turns rational adults into rigid defenders.

The Pointer

Frame around protection and future gain.

You cannot eliminate loss aversion—but you can work with it.

The seasoned negotiator reframes conversations to reduce perceived loss and highlight protection. Instead of: "You're behind schedule." Try: "We need to protect the milestone. What adjustments help us recover without burning your crew?"

Instead of: "This is your change." Try: "Here's what shifted from the original scope. Let's walk through how to address it without either of us absorbing unintended cost." Notice the shift. The language protects identity and signals partnership in avoiding loss. Three practical tactics help on the job-site:

1. Make losses private, not public. Correct in one-on-one settings. Praise in meetings. Public exposure amplifies perceived loss.
2. Separate sunk cost from future cost. Ask: "If we were starting today, would we still do it this way?" This reframes from defending past loss to optimizing future gain.
3. Quantify prevention, not just expense. When presenting a cost, link it to avoided loss. "This adjustment prevents a two-week delay downstream." Now the conversation is about avoiding a bigger loss—not accepting a smaller one.

Another powerful tool is pre-commitment. Early in a

project, align on shared loss thresholds:

- "If weather impacts exceed X days, we revisit schedule."
- "If steel pricing moves beyond Y%, we reopen procurement terms."

Pre-alignment reduces the emotional spike when adjustments occur because expectations were set. Most importantly, protect dignity.

On a job-site, reputation travels faster than concrete cures. When someone feels publicly diminished, recovery is slow. The skilled leader preserves face while solving problems.

Loss aversion is not weakness. It is wiring. On the job-site, where margins are thin and reputations visible, losses feel amplified. If you ignore that, you trigger defensiveness. If you weaponize it, you damage relationships. But if you understand it, you gain leverage without aggression. The negotiator who reduces perceived loss often gains the outcome, because when people feel protected, they collaborate. And collaboration is worth more than any single concession

INSIGHT 52 – REACTIVE DEVALUATION

In negotiation, value is rarely judged on substance alone. It is filtered through perception. And one of the most powerful distortions in that filter is reactive devaluation.

Reactive devaluation is the tendency to discount an idea, proposal, or concession simply because it comes from the other side. If they offer it, we assume it must favor them. If they agree too quickly, we suspect a trap. If they suggest a compromise, we wonder what we're missing. The proposal hasn't changed. The math hasn't changed. Only the source has changed. Yet suddenly the value feels smaller.

This bias operates quietly - but it derails deals, prolongs disputes, and hardens positions that might otherwise have softened.

Let's break it down.

The Principle

We judge offers by who makes them, not just what they contain.

Reactive devaluation is rooted in mistrust and identity protection. When someone we perceive as an opponent offers a concession, our instinct is to protect ourselves. We assume they wouldn't suggest something unless it benefits them disproportionately.

So, we discount it. Ironically, this bias often activates at the very moment progress becomes possible. A contractor proposes splitting unforeseen costs. A supplier suggests expedited shipping at reduced margin. A project owner offers a scheduling adjustment that protects everyone's exposure. Instead of recognizing movement, the other side thinks: "If they're offering this, it must not be that valuable."

And so, they push for more. Reactive devaluation is strongest when:

- Trust is low.
- Stakes are high.
- Identity feels threatened.
- The relationship has prior tension.

The more adversarial the context, the more heavily proposals are discounted. The seasoned negotiator understands this. Progress often gets rejected not because it's bad, but because it came from the wrong mouth. That means the work is not just crafting the right offer. It's managing how that offer will be perceived. Value must sometimes be separated from the identity of the proposer.

The Pitfall

Mistaking suspicion for strength.

Many negotiators believe skepticism equals leverage. So, when the other side offers something meaningful, they instinctively resist accepting it too quickly. They worry that agreement signals weakness. They fear being "taken." This reflex creates three problems.

First, it escalates unnecessarily. An offer intended as a bridge becomes a new battleground. The proposing party feels punished for moving first and withdraws generosity in future rounds.

Second, it hardens identity. Once a concession is rejected, it is psychologically harder to re-offer it. Pride and face become involved. What could have been progress turns into entrenchment.

Third, it distorts objective evaluation. Instead of asking, "Is this good for us?" the question becomes, "Why would they offer this?" Suspicion replaces analysis.

On a job site, this often plays out when a foreman proposes a change order compromise to keep work moving. The owner, assuming hidden margin padding, rejects it outright. Work slows. Costs rise. The original proposal, now retrospectively reasonable, disappears.

Reactive devaluation doesn't protect value. It often destroys it. The deeper pitfall is believing that resistance automatically creates better outcomes. Sometimes it simply eliminates the best one available.

The Pointer

Separate the offer from the opponent

To counter reactive devaluation, you must slow the instinct to judge by source. When you receive a proposal, ask three disciplined questions:

1. If this exact offer came from a neutral third party, how would I evaluate it?
2. How does this compare objectively to our alternatives?
3. What interests of ours does this meaningfully address?

This reframes evaluation around substance instead of suspicion. There are also strategic ways to reduce reactive devaluation when you are the one making the offer.

Invite joint authorship. Instead of presenting a fully formed solution, build it collaboratively: "What if we structured it this way?" or "How would this land for you?" When people help shape a proposal, they devalue it less.

Use objective standards. Anchor concessions in data, benchmarks, industry norms, or prior agreements. The more an offer appears grounded in shared standards, the less it feels like a tactical maneuver.

Let them suggest it. Sometimes the most effective move is to guide the conversation so the other side proposes the compromise you had in mind. An idea feels more valuable when it originates internally.

And perhaps most importantly: Acknowledge the psychology directly. In tense negotiations, it can be powerful to say: "I know when something comes from us, it may feel like there's a catch. Let's slow it down and evaluate the merits together." Naming the bias reduces its power.

Reactive devaluation is not about math. It is about mistrust. When identity and ego are activated, the brain looks for threat, even inside opportunity. The disciplined negotiator resists this reflex. They understand that progress often arrives disguised as an opponent's concession. They know that rejecting movement simply because it came from the other side is not strength - it is insecurity.

Negotiation maturity means being able to say: "This helps us. It doesn't matter who suggested it." The goal is not to win authorship of every idea. The goal is to reach durable agreement.

When you learn to evaluate proposals on merit rather than origin, you reduce unnecessary escalation, preserve relationships, and capture value that others walk away from out of pride.

Reactive devaluation whispers, "Don't trust it." Wisdom replies, "Examine it." And that pause, the space between reflex and reason, is where better agreements are made.

INSIGHT 53 – EGO INVESTMENT

In negotiation and conflict, we like to think we are defending logic, fairness, and sound judgment. In reality, we are often defending something far more fragile: our identity. When a proposal becomes my idea, when a decision becomes my call, when a position

becomes tied to my credibility, the conversation is no longer about the issue. It is about ego investment.

Ego investment is not arrogance. It is attachment. It happens when our sense of competence, authority, intelligence, or status becomes entangled with a particular outcome. And once that happens, flexibility feels like humiliation.

Understanding ego investment is essential for anyone who leads, negotiates, or works in high-stakes environments where decisions carry consequences and visibility.

The Principle

People defend identity more than ideas.

Ego investment reflects a simple psychological truth: people protect their identity with more intensity than they protect their logic.

When someone challenges a proposal, it may feel like they are challenging competence. When they question an assumption, it may feel like they are questioning judgment. When they suggest an alternative, it may feel like they are rewriting authorship.

Once identity is at stake, the brain shifts from collaborative reasoning to defensive posture. The conversation tightens. Listening narrows. The objective subtly changes from "What's best?" to "How do I avoid losing face?"

This dynamic is amplified in visible leadership roles. The superintendent who recommended a schedule, the project manager who selected a vendor, the executive who announced a strategy—all of them carry reputational weight. Backtracking feels costly.

Ego investment also escalates over time. The longer someone publicly advocates a position, the more psychologically expensive it becomes to change it. The sunk cost is not financial; it is reputational.

Ironically, the stronger the ego investment, the harder it becomes to see risk clearly. Data that threatens identity is discounted. Dissent is interpreted as disloyalty. Neutral feedback feels adversarial.

The principle is this: When identity fuses with position, rational flexibility decreases. The most effective negotiators and leaders recognize that ego investment is inevitable—but manageable. They separate "being right" from "getting it right."

The Pitfall

Doubling down to protect image.

The most common pitfall of ego investment is escalation through defense. When someone is invested in a decision, even small challenges can feel like large threats. Instead of examining new information, they reinforce the original stance. They gather confirming data. They dismiss dissenters. They restate the argument with greater certainty.

The goal shifts from solving the problem to preserving authority. This doubling down often happens subtly. A leader may say, "We've already committed," when the real concern is, "If we reverse course, I look weak." A negotiator may reject a reasonable concession because accepting it implies their initial demand was inflated. Ego-driven rigidity can create avoidable losses:

- Continuing a flawed plan to avoid admitting error.
- Rejecting a mutually beneficial compromise.
- Damaging relationships by treating disagreement as disrespect.
- Silencing valuable input from team members.

On job sites, in boardrooms, or in contract discussions, this pitfall is particularly costly. Construction projects, for example, demand constant recalibration. Weather shifts. Supply chains change. Design assumptions evolve. A leader overly attached to an earlier plan can drive a project into unnecessary delay or cost overruns simply to avoid appearing inconsistent.

Ego investment also poisons culture. When people observe that leaders cannot change their minds without losing face, they stop offering candid input. Innovation declines. Risk rises.

The deeper danger is internal. When ego investment

dominates, leaders start believing their own defense. They convince themselves that changing course would indeed signal incompetence, when in reality adaptability signals strength.

The Pointer

Protect dignity, not position.

The key to managing ego investment is not to eliminate pride or confidence. It is to shift what you are protecting. Protect dignity, not position.

Dignity is preserved through integrity, openness, and accountability. Position is preserved through rigidity and defensiveness.

One practical tool is language reframing. Instead of saying, "I was wrong," which feels like identity collapse, say, "New information has changed the landscape." Instead of, "That won't work," say, "Help me understand how this improves on our current approach." These shifts allow movement without humiliation.

Another powerful practice is pre-commitment to adaptability. At the outset of major decisions, say publicly, "This is our best call based on what we know today. If new data emerges, we'll adjust." That statement separates identity from outcome before ego has time to attach.

Invite dissent early. Ask explicitly, "What are we missing?" When criticism is normalized, it feels less like attack and more like collaboration.

In negotiation, detach authorship from evaluation. If someone challenges your proposal, respond to the content, not the implied critique. A calm "Let's test that" diffuses ego friction.

When you sense ego investment rising, a tight jaw, an elevated tone, defensiveness, pause. Ask yourself privately:

"Am I defending the solution, or am I defending myself?" That moment of awareness creates space for choice.

Finally, give others exit ramps. If someone else is ego-invested, don't corner them. Provide a dignified path to adjustment. Frame alternatives as refinements rather than reversals. Publicly credit their earlier contribution before suggesting evolution. People rarely resist better ideas; they resist losing status.

Ego investment is not a character flaw. It is a human reflex. In environments where reputation, authority, and competence matter, attachment to decisions is natural. But strong leadership is not measured by the ability to hold a line at all costs. It is measured by the ability to pivot without losing credibility.

The mature negotiator understands this distinction. They recognize that being respected is more durable than being right. They value learning over winning. They understand that flexibility, handled well, increases trust rather than diminishing it.

When you separate your identity from your ideas, you gain a powerful advantage. You can change course quickly. You can listen without threat. You can adapt without shame.

And in negotiation, and leadership, that freedom is strength.

INSIGHT 54 – OVERCONFIDENCE IN EXPERIENCE

Experience is powerful. It is earned the hard way, through failed bids, blown schedules, tense mediations, and contracts that almost collapsed under pressure. Over time, experience becomes instinct. And instinct becomes speed. But speed, in negotiation, can quietly

become blindness.

The more seasoned you become, the more vulnerable you are to believing you've "seen this before." And once you believe that, you stop truly seeing what's in front of you.

The Principle

Experience is pattern recognition - not pattern certainty.

Experience works because it builds mental shortcuts. A seasoned negotiator walks into a room and quickly reads power dynamics, emotional temperature, and leverage positions. You recognize the telltale signs: the defensive posture, the inflated first demand, the sudden silence before an ultimatum. Pattern recognition is not arrogance. It is efficiency. But here is the distinction: experience identifies patterns; it does not guarantee this is the same pattern.

The danger begins when recognition turns into assumption. You've handled dozens of subcontractor disputes. You've renegotiated supply contracts during shortages. You've mediated labor grievances that looked exactly like this one. Your brain whispers, "I know how this plays out." That whisper is comforting. It is also risky.

Overconfidence in experience leads you to categorize too quickly. You stop asking fresh questions. You filter new information through old conclusions. You interpret behavior based on prior cases rather than current facts. Experience should sharpen curiosity, not replace it.

The seasoned negotiator understands that every negotiation has familiar elements, but no two negotiations are identical. Markets shift. Personalities differ. Incentives evolve. What worked five years ago, or even last quarter, may misfire today. Experience gives you hypotheses. It does not give you permission to stop testing them.

The Pitfall

Mistaking familiarity for mastery.

Overconfidence rarely looks loud. It often shows up as subtle dismissal. You hear a proposal and think, that won't work. You see resistance and assume, they're posturing. You encounter silence and conclude, they'll fold.

The problem is not that these interpretations are impossible. The problem is that you stop verifying them. The experienced negotiator is especially vulnerable because success reinforces certainty. If your instincts have been right before, you begin to trust them more than the process.

You prepare less thoroughly because "this is straightforward." You listen less carefully because "I already know their angle." You probe less deeply because, "I've solved this type of problem before."

Familiarity creates cognitive compression. You reduce a complex situation to a known template. Templates are efficient. Until they are wrong.

In construction, a veteran project executive may assume a schedule dispute is purely about money because that's how it has played out dozens of times. But this time, the subcontractor's issue is reputational risk or internal politics. If you negotiate strictly on dollars, you miss the actual lever.

In labor relations, you might assume hardline rhetoric is positioning for a predictable midpoint compromise. But perhaps the membership vote is closer than leadership admits, and flexibility is truly limited. If you push expecting collapse, you may trigger escalation instead. Overconfidence creates three specific distortions:

1. Under-preparation - "We've done this before."
2. Premature closure - "I know what they want."
3. Dismissed anomalies - "That's just noise."

The irony? The more experienced you are, the more dangerous these distortions become because others assume you must be right. And often, no one challenges the veteran in the room.

The Pointer

Replace certainty with structured curiosity.

The antidote to overconfidence is not doubt in your competence, it is discipline in your inquiry. Seasoned negotiators build guardrails against their own expertise.

First, they deliberately generate alternative explanations. If you believe the other side is bluffing, ask: What if they're not? What would make this demand real? If you assume price is the issue, ask, what non-monetary risk might be driving this?

Second, they prepare as if they were new to the problem. That doesn't mean ignoring experience. It means refusing to let it shorten preparation. They still map stakeholders, pressures, timelines, and unseen constraints - even if the surface structure looks familiar.

Third, they invite disconfirming input. They ask a colleague, "What am I missing, where might I be wrong?" They look for data that contradicts their early impressions instead of reinforcing them.

Fourth, they slow down key assumptions in the room. Instead of declaring, "We know how this ends," they say, "Help me understand what makes this situation different from the last one." This posture does not weaken authority. It strengthens it. That's because humility in experience signals confidence, not insecurity.

The seasoned negotiator recognizes that experience is a powerful lens, but lenses can distort. So, they clean it. They adjust it. They re-focus it. They do not throw it away.

Experience should make you sharper, not more rigid. Faster, not more careless. More perceptive, not more presumptive.

There is a quiet strength in saying, even after decades in the field, "I've seen something like this before, but I want to understand what makes this one unique." That sentence protects you from complacency. It keeps you alert to nuance. It keeps you negotiating the situation in front of you, not the one from five years ago.

Overconfidence in experience does not usually cause dramatic failure. It causes subtle misreads. Small missed signals. Gradual erosion of leverage because you stopped noticing change. And in high-stakes negotiations, subtle misreads compound.

Experience is an asset, but only when it remains a tool not an identity. The moment you begin negotiating to defend your reputation as "the one who knows," you are no longer reading the room. You are protecting your ego.

Negotiation punishes ego more reliably than inexperience. The seasoned professional does not rely on experience alone. They interrogate it. That is the difference between having years in the field and continuing to grow in it.

INSIGHT 55 – THE PRESSURE OF CONSTITUENTS

Negotiations are rarely two-sided. They only look that way from across the table.

In reality, most negotiations are triangular. You sit across from "the other side," but you stand on behalf of people who are not in the room - executives, board members, labor crews, voters, partners, shareholders, family members. They are your constituents. They shape what you can say, what you can concede, and what you must defend.

And they are often louder in your head than the person in front of you.

The seasoned negotiator understands this invisible pressure, not only in themselves, but in the other side. Managing constituents is often more important than managing terms.

The Principle

Every negotiation is a two-level game.

Political scientist Robert Putnam famously described negotiation as a "two-level game." You negotiate externally at the table and internally with your own stakeholders. A deal that works across the table but fails at home or the office is not a deal at all.

A superintendent negotiating a schedule adjustment may personally see the logic in a compromise. But if the field crew believes management is "giving away leverage," resistance builds. A labor leader may understand the contractor's financial constraints but must answer to members who demand visible wins. A CEO may agree privately on risk allocation but face a board that demands aggressive protection. The principle is simple: You are never negotiating for yourself alone. Every offer you make must survive two approvals:

1. The party across the table.
2. The party behind you.

If either rejects it, the agreement collapses. This creates pressure. You may feel boxed in by expectations, performance optics, or fear of appearing weak. The other side feels the same. The mistake is assuming rigidity equals hostility. Often, it just equals audience.

The Pitfall

Negotiating for applause instead of agreement.

Under constituent pressure, negotiators begin performing. They posture. They overstate positions. They reject reasonable proposals too quickly. They escalate language. They demand visible concessions rather than practical solutions. Why? Because someone is watching.

In construction, this shows up when a project executive

refuses to concede a minor point because "corporate is tracking this job closely." In labor negotiations, it appears when a spokesperson hardens their tone before membership votes. In public disputes, leaders speak to cameras rather than to each other.

The negotiation becomes theater.

The pitfall is subtle: instead of asking, "What solves the problem?" the negotiator asks, "How will this look?"

When optics dominate substance, progress slows. Parties entrench to prove loyalty to their base. Even small compromises feel like betrayal. Offers are rejected not because they're insufficient, but because they're politically dangerous. This is how rational actors become publicly unreasonable.

And here's the deeper danger: constituent pressure narrows perceived authority. Negotiators tell themselves, "I don't have room," even when creative options exist. They hide behind invisible constraints. Sometimes the constraints are real. Often, they are assumed.

The Pointer

Negotiate the room behind the room.

The seasoned negotiator does three things differently.

First, they map the constituencies on both sides. Before arguing terms, they identify audiences.

- Who must approve this?
- Who feels threatened by change?
- Who gains status from hardline positions?
- Who has veto power, formally or informally? Second, they create face-saving pathways.
- If the other side needs to show strength, structure concessions so they can claim value.
- Break agreements into components so each side

can "win" visibly somewhere.
- Frame compromises as joint problem-solving rather than capitulation.

Instead of saying, "You need to move," say, "How do we structure this so you can defend it internally?" That question alone changes the tone.

Third, they manage their own constituents proactively. They do not negotiate externally and explain later. They prepare their people in advance. They say:

- "There may be trade-offs."
- "If we gain X, we may concede Y."
- "Our goal is long-term stability, not short-term optics."

By shaping expectations early, they reduce backlash later. When internal stakeholders are surprised, they revolt. When they are prepared, they support. This is leadership inside negotiation.

Understanding constituent pressure gives you leverage - not manipulative leverage, but strategic leverage. When someone says, "I can't accept that," ask yourself, Can't? Or can't sell it?

Those are different problems. If the issue is salability, you can redesign presentation. You can adjust sequencing. You can provide cover. You can offer language that helps them explain.

Many stalled negotiations are not blocked by substance. They are blocked by explain ability. The seasoned negotiator listens for phrases like:

- "My board won't go for that."
- "My crew will never accept this."
- "I don't have authority."

These are not dead ends. They are signals. They reveal

where the real negotiation must occur.

Sometimes the smartest move is a caucus - giving the other side space to consult their stakeholders without losing face. Sometimes it's proposing a pilot program rather than a permanent shift. Sometimes it's allowing them to announce the agreement in their own framing. You are not just building an agreement. You are building an agreement that can survive scrutiny.

The pressure of constituents is unavoidable. The question is whether it controls you or informs you. When you ignore it, you become frustrated by rigidity. When you fear it, you overcompensate with aggression. When you understand it, you design around it.

Negotiation is not only about solving problems between two parties. It is about aligning systems of accountability. The mature negotiator does not resent the invisible audience. They respect it, because in the end, the deal is not finished when hands are shaken. It is finished when it is ratified, implemented, and defended in rooms you may never see.

And the negotiator who learns to manage the pressure behind the table gains something more powerful than tactical advantage. They gain durability. That is what separates agreements that collapse under criticism from those that endure under pressure.

INSIGHT 56 – IDENTITY-BASED CONFLICT

Not every negotiation is about money, schedule, or scope. Some are about who someone believes they are. Identity-based conflict occurs when a disagreement threatens a person's sense of competence, status, role, values, or belonging. When identity is

involved, logic alone will not solve the problem, because logic is not what is being defended.

A superintendent arguing over sequencing may not be fighting about sequencing at all. He may be fighting to protect his reputation as someone who "runs a tight job." A union leader resisting a proposal may not be focused on the numbers; she may be protecting her credibility with her members. A senior executive rejecting a suggestion may feel their authority is being eroded.

When identity feels threatened, the nervous system reacts before the intellect does. The conversation shifts from problem-solving to self-protection. Understanding this distinction changes everything.

The Principle

When identity is threatened, the conflict escalates.

When identity is affirmed, the conflict stabilizes. People defend who they are before they defend what they want. Identity is tied to:

- Competence ("I know what I'm doing.")
- Authority ("I'm the decision-maker.")
- Fairness ("I stand for what's right.")
- Loyalty ("I protect my people.")
- Experience ("I've been doing this for 30 years.")

If a proposal implies incompetence, disrespect, or irrelevance, resistance will intensify, regardless of how reasonable the proposal is. This is why negotiations sometimes become inexplicably heated. A minor correction feels like a public demotion. A simple question feels like an accusation. A data point feels like an attack.

Identity-based conflict is rarely announced directly. It shows up as rigidity, sarcasm, escalation, or moral framing. Instead of "This won't work," you hear, "That's ridiculous." Instead of "I disagree," you hear, "You don't understand how this business works."

The seasoned negotiator listens for the identity underneath the argument. They ask themselves:

- What role is this person protecting?
- What status feels at risk?
- What value feels challenged?

When you address identity, the temperature drops. When you ignore it, the temperature rises. Affirmation does not mean agreement. It means recognizing legitimacy in the other person's role or perspective.

"You've been running jobs longer than I've been in the business." "I understand why your members would see it that way." "You're accountable for this outcome. I respect that."

Those statements cost nothing—and often unlock everything.

The Pitfall

Arguing substance when the real fight is about status.

The most common mistake in identity-based conflict is doubling down on facts. When someone reacts strongly, the instinct is to explain more clearly, provide more evidence, or press harder. But if the other party feels diminished, additional logic sounds like additional disrespect.

Facts without affirmation feel like correction. Correction without context feels like humiliation.

Consider a job-site scenario: A project manager points out errors in a subcontractor's work in front of the crew. The PM may be factually correct. But if the subcontractor experiences that moment as a public loss of face, the dispute will not remain technical. It becomes personal.

From that point forward, cooperation declines. Emails get sharper. Delays multiply. Every minor issue becomes a battlefield. The conflict expands because identity is now on trial.

Another common pitfall is moral escalation. When identity is threatened, people frame their position as a matter of principle: "This is about integrity." "This is about respect." "This is about fairness." The danger is that moral language hardens compromise. Once something becomes a referendum on character, backing down feels like self-betrayal. The more someone feels judged, the less flexible they become.

Negotiators who miss this dynamic often label the other side as "difficult," "irrational," or "ego-driven." But labeling intensifies the very threat that is driving the behavior. Identity-based conflict is not about ego in the shallow sense. It is about dignity and dignity is non-negotiable.

The Pointer

Protect dignity first. Solve the problem second.

The seasoned negotiator separates identity from issue before attempting resolution. They lower the threat level by:

- Acknowledging experience.
- Validating responsibility.
- Recognizing constraints.
- Respecting authority structures.

This is not flattery. It is strategic stabilization.

For example: Instead of: "You're wrong about the schedule impact," try, "You've been managing this sequencing since day one. Help me understand how you're seeing the impact differently than we are."

Instead of, "This proposal doesn't make sense," try, "I know you're trying to protect your members here. Let's look at what protects them and still keeps the project viable."

Notice the difference. The second approach preserves role and competence. It invites collaboration rather than competition. Another powerful move is shifting the conversation from "Who's right?" to "What does the role require?" When identity is anchored to role rather than ego, flexibility increases. "What does your position require you to protect?" "What are you accountable for here?" These questions allow someone to stand firm on responsibility without standing rigid on posture.

Finally, be mindful of public settings. Identity threats multiply in front of audiences. If correction or challenge is necessary, consider moving it to a private forum. Preserve face wherever possible. In high-stakes negotiations, small gestures of respect yield disproportionate returns.

Identity-based conflict does not disappear through force. It dissolves through recognition. When people feel seen in their role, respected in their responsibility, and secure in their competence, they become far more willing to explore solutions.

The goal is not to win the argument. The goal is to maintain the relationship while resolving the issue. Once identity is defended, the conversation can return to substance and substance is where progress lives.

INSIGHT 57 – FEAR OF APPEARING WEAK

Every negotiation has two conversations happening at once. One is about substance, money, scope, timelines, and risk. The other is about status, who is strong, who is in control, and who is backing down.

The fear of appearing weak lives in that second conversation. It is rarely spoken aloud, but it drives more bad decisions than lack of preparation ever does.

This insight explores the principle behind that fear, the pitfall it creates, and the pointer that separates seasoned negotiators from insecure ones.

The Principle

Strength is not the absence of concession - it is control of movement.

In negotiation, weakness is not defined by flexibility. It is defined by loss of control. Strong negotiators understand that movement is inevitable. No serious agreement happens without adjustment. The question is not whether you move. The question is whether you move deliberately or reactively.

When people fear appearing weak, they equate concession with surrender. They assume that any shift signals vulnerability. So, they anchor themselves rigidly to initial positions—even when those positions are inefficient or unsustainable. But rigidity is not strength. It is anxiety in disguise.

True strength lies in disciplined flexibility. It is the ability to move without losing frame. It is making concessions that are conditional, sequenced, and purposeful. It is saying, "If we adjust here, we need movement there."

Strength is measured by whether you shape the negotiation's direction—not whether you refuse to bend. The seasoned negotiator knows that refusing to move can feel powerful in the moment. But shaping the movement is what produces durable agreements.

Strength is not volume. Strength is not stubbornness. Strength is controlled progression.

The Pitfall

Posturing to protect image.

The fear of appearing weak leads to posturing and posturing shows up in several predictable ways:

- Overstating certainty.
- Rejecting reasonable proposals too quickly.

- Escalating tone to demonstrate resolve.
- Refusing to ask clarifying questions.
- Withholding information that could unlock value.

The logic behind posturing is simple: if I project confidence aggressively enough, no one will test me. But posturing creates three hidden costs.

First, it narrows information flow. When you posture, others become guarded. They stop sharing data. And without information, you negotiate blind.

Second, it escalates ego investment. Once you've declared a position forcefully, walking it back feels humiliating. Now the issue is no longer the substance—it is your identity.

Third, it traps you in performative toughness. You begin negotiating for the audience instead of the outcome. In high-stakes environments, boardrooms, union negotiations, executive contracts, jobsite disputes, the fear of appearing weak is amplified by observers. Constituents are watching. Teams are listening. Reputations feel exposed.

And so, leaders double down.

The harder you try to look strong, the more fragile your position becomes. This is because your flexibility is now constrained by optics. Seasoned negotiators understand that image management is part of the game, but they do not let it run the game. They recognize that appearing reasonable often increases leverage, not diminishes it.

The Pointer

Redefine strength as strategic transparency.

The practical shift is this: redefine what strength looks like in your own mind before you walk into the room. If you define strength as dominance, you will overplay your hand. If you define strength as composure and clarity, you will negotiate differently.

Strategic transparency is one of the most powerful tools available to a negotiator who refuses to be ruled by insecurity. Strategic transparency does not mean revealing everything. It means calmly naming constraints, priorities, and decision logic without defensiveness. For example:

- “Here’s where our margin pressure is.”
- “This timeline exposes us to risk.”
- “We have authority to move on structure, not total cost.”

These statements are not weak. They are grounding. They shift the negotiation from a contest of egos to a problem-solving frame.

Another pointer: separate your personal identity from the proposal. When someone challenges your offer, they are not challenging your competence. They are responding to incentives. If you internalize every counteroffer as disrespect, you will fight to defend yourself rather than improve the deal.

Ask yourself quietly: Am I resisting this because it’s bad for the agreement, or because it feels bad for me?

Finally, use conditional movement as a strength signal. Instead of saying, “Fine, we’ll do it,” say, “If we can resolve the inspection timing, we can adjust price.”

Instead of retreating silently, say, “We can move here, but we’ll need assurance on that.”

You are not backing down. You are structuring exchange. The difference is subtle, but it is decisive.

The fear of appearing weak is rooted in a very human concern: status. No one wants to lose face. No leader wants to look unsure. No negotiator wants to seem outmatched. Negotiation is not a performance of invincibility. It is a disciplined process of exchange under uncertainty.

Weakness is not measured by movement. It is measured by emotional reactivity.

When fear governs you, you cling. When confidence governs you, you calibrate.

The seasoned negotiator understands this. Appearing reasonable is often the strongest position in the room. Flexibility, when structured and deliberate, signals control, not fragility. And in the end, the party who controls the movement controls the outcome.

INSIGHT 58 – THE DISCIPLINE OF PERSPECTIVE

Perspective is one of the most underappreciated disciplines in negotiation. It is often mistaken for empathy, patience, or simple listening. In reality, it is something more deliberate and demanding. Perspective is the intentional effort to understand how the situation

looks from the other side of the table, not just what they are saying, but why they are saying it, what pressures they carry, and what risks they believe they face.

Most negotiators enter a discussion with clarity about their own interests, constraints, and objectives. They know what outcome they need, what authority they have, and what consequences follow if the negotiation fails. What they often lack is an equally disciplined understanding of the other side's reality. Without that, every action taken by the other party can appear irrational, stubborn, or unnecessarily difficult.

But in most cases, the other side is not behaving irrationally at all. They are responding to incentives, fears, obligations, and expectations that may not be visible from across the table.

The seasoned negotiator understands something simple and powerful: perspective is leverage.

The Principle

Perspective expands the field.

The first principle of perspective is this: The way you frame the situation determines the range of solutions you can see. When you see a conflict only as a pricing issue, you argue numbers. When you see it as a schedule issue, you argue timelines. But when you discipline yourself to step back, you may discover it is actually about risk, authority, reputation, or fear of loss.

Perspective expands the field. On a job-site, a subcontractor may insist on a change order that feels unreasonable. From your vantage point, it looks like opportunism. From theirs, it may look like survival. They may be carrying thin margins, labor shortages, and exposure they cannot afford. If you stay locked in your own framing, "They're trying to squeeze us"—you will respond with resistance. If you widen the frame, "What pressure are they under?"—you respond with curiosity.

That shift does not mean you concede. It means you understand. Perspective allows you to separate intent from impact. It prevents you from personalizing what may simply be structural pressure. It transforms the negotiation from a clash of wills into a problem to be examined.

When perspective expands, creativity follows. The disciplined negotiator asks:

- What does this look like from their seat?
- What risk are they trying to reduce?
- What loss are they trying to avoid?
- What constraint am I underestimating?

These questions stretch the frame. And a stretched frame makes rigid positions harder to maintain.

The Pitfall

Perspective collapse.

The pitfall is what happens under pressure when perspective collapses. Deadlines loom. Stakeholders push. Money is at risk. Under stress, the brain narrows its field of vision. It defaults to certainty. It assumes motives. It simplifies the story: "They're being unreasonable." "They don't respect us." "They always do this." This is not analysis. It is compression.

Perspective collapse creates false binaries, win or lose, strong or weak, right or wrong. It blinds you to nuance. And once you adopt a compressed view, you begin to behave in ways that confirm it. Tone sharpens. Listening fades. Questions become accusations.

In construction negotiations, perspective collapse often shows up when a project goes sideways. Delays begin to stack up. Costs rise. Emails harden. Each side builds a narrative of blame. And the more energy invested in that narrative, the harder it becomes to step outside it.

The danger is not just relational. It is strategic. When perspective collapses, you miss information. You ignore signals that could lead to resolution. You mistake surface positions for core interests. You negotiate against a caricature rather than a complex human reality.

And the most dangerous form of collapse? Moral certainty.

When you are convinced, you are entirely right, you stop being curious. And when curiosity disappears, progress stalls.

The Pointer

Build the muscle before you need it.

Perspective is not something you access only in crisis. It is a muscle you build before the pressure hits. The practical pointer is this: Create deliberate pauses that force perspective widening.

Before responding to a hard demand, write down three plausible explanations for why the other side is acting this way. Not one. Three. This forces your mind beyond the most convenient narrative.

In tense meetings, summarize the other side's position in a way they agree is accurate. Not softened. Not reframed to your advantage. Accurate. This does two things: it lowers defensiveness and tests whether you truly understand their vantage point.

In preparation, ask: "If I were advising them, what would I tell them to demand?" This single question sharpens your anticipation and expands your field.

On a job-site, when tempers rise, step physically aside if you can. Change posture. Slow your breathing. The body influences perspective more often than we admit. A regulated nervous system sees more clearly than an agitated one.

And perhaps most importantly: distinguish between understanding and agreement. Many leaders resist perspective because they equate it with concession. It is not. Understanding gives you more precise influence. It allows you to respond to the real pressure rather than the visible posture.

The seasoned negotiator can articulate the other side's concerns better than they can themselves. That ability is not weakness. It is strategic strength.

Perspective does not mean abandoning your own interests. It means situating them within a broader map. When you see the terrain more fully, you make fewer tactical errors. You avoid unnecessary escalations. You uncover trades that were invisible when your view was narrow.

The discipline of perspective requires humility. It requires slowing down when urgency demands speed. It requires resisting the emotional reward of certainty. But its payoff is significant. Perspective keeps relationships intact under strain. It reveals hidden variables. It prevents miscalculation. It turns adversaries into counterparts.

In the end, negotiation is rarely defeated by lack of intelligence. It is defeated by lack of range. The disciplined leader widens the lens, again and again, until the problem is seen in full dimension. When perspective expands, possibility does too.

CHAPTER SEVEN

LEADERSHIP IN NEGOTIATION

"Understand that credibility is not something you declare; it is something others conclude."

Insight 59. The Seasoned Negotiator's Mindset

Insight 60. Emotional Regulation as Professional Skill

Insight 61. Building Credibility Over Time

Insight 62. The Value of Teaching Negotiation to Field Leaders

Insight 63. Consensus vs. Command Decisions

Insight 64. Strategic Patience

Insight 65. Knowing When to Escalate

Insight 66. Knowing When to De-Escalate

Insight 67. Institutional Memory and Reputation

Insight 68. Negotiation as Stewardship

INSIGHT 59 – THE SEASONED NEGOTIATOR'S MINDSET

Negotiation is not a performance. It is not a contest of clever lines or dramatic wins. It is a discipline of thinking under pressure.

The seasoned negotiator is not defined by charisma, volume, or aggression. He or she is defined by mindset, by the internal structure that shapes how conflict is interpreted, how risk is assessed, and how emotion is managed. While amateurs focus on tactics, veterans focus on orientation. Because what you believe about negotiation determines how you behave inside it. This inner posture separates experience from wisdom.

The Principle

Negotiation is a thinking exercise under pressure.

The seasoned negotiator understands that negotiation is primarily cognitive, not theatrical. It is the disciplined practice of staying oriented when others become reactive.

When talks intensify, deadlines compress, voices rise, and constituencies apply pressure, the inexperienced negotiator feels urgency as a command. Act now. Concede something. Escalate. Push back harder.

The seasoned negotiator feels urgency as data. They know that pressure distorts perception. It narrows focus, exaggerates threats, and tempts shortcuts. So instead of reacting to the heat, they regulate it internally. They ask:

- What problem are we actually solving?
- What assumptions are driving this tension?
- What part of this is signal, and what part is emotion?
- Who truly has authority here?
- What happens if we do nothing for a moment? This mindset is anchored in three quiet convictions:

1. Most conflict is about perception before it is about substance.
2. Time pressure is often psychological, not structural.
3. Emotion is information, not instruction.

A seasoned negotiator does not rush to speak. They rush to understand. They resist the seduction of being the smartest voice in the room. Instead, they discipline themselves to be the clearest thinker in the room. And clarity, not dominance, is what creates leverage.

The Pitfall

Confusing experience with immunity.

Experience can be a teacher - or a trap. The pitfall is believing that because you have negotiated many times, you are immune to bias, ego, or escalation. In reality, familiarity often breeds overconfidence. You begin to assume you've "seen this before." You categorize too quickly. You diagnose too fast.

The danger is subtle. You stop listening for nuance. You assume the other side's motives. You predict their next move and negotiate against your own prediction instead of their actual words. The seasoned negotiator's greatest vulnerability is complacency.

Another version of this pitfall is identity attachment. After years of successful negotiations, reputation becomes intertwined with outcome. You are no longer simply solving a problem; you are defending your image as a strong, savvy dealmaker.

Now the negotiation is no longer about terms. It is about you. And once ego is on the table, flexibility disappears. Concessions feel like losses. Questions feel like weakness. Silence feels dangerous. Ironically, the more experienced someone is, the more disciplined they must become about intellectual humility. Mindset is not something you achieve once. It is something you maintain.

The Pointer

Think in horizons, not moments.

The seasoned negotiator does not think in exchanges. They think in trajectories. Amateurs focus on the current statement: "What did they just demand?" "What did we just concede?"

Veterans focus on direction: "Where is this conversation heading?" "What pattern is forming?" "What will this look like in six months?"

This shift changes everything. When you think in moments, you react. When you think in horizons, you shape. A demand that feels aggressive in the moment may be a testing probe in the larger arc. A concession that feels costly today may buy relational capital tomorrow. A pause that feels risky now may prevent a structural mistake later. The seasoned mindset asks a different set of questions:

- Is this a short-term victory or a long-term advantage?
- Are we solving the right problem, or just relieving immediate tension?
- What precedent are we setting?
- What story will each side talk about when this negotiation has ended?

This forward orientation stabilizes decision-making. It also cultivates emotional steadiness. Because when you see beyond the immediate flare-up, today's conflict feels less catastrophic. You are not trying to "win this round." You are shaping an enduring outcome.

The seasoned negotiator's mindset is built on four internal disciplines:

1. 1. Detachment without disengagement. Care about the outcome but do not fuse your

identity to it.

2. Curiosity before certainty. Assume there is information you do not yet see.
3. Pacing over pressure. Slow the conversation when others speed it up.
4. Long-term credibility over short-term dominance. Protect reputation by being steady, not spectacular.

Notice what is absent: manipulation, theatrics, intimidation. The seasoned negotiator does not rely on clever tricks. They rely on composure. They understand that mindset is contagious. If you remain calm, structured, and deliberate, the room often follows. If you become reactive, the room fractures. The greatest leverage in negotiation is not a tactic; it is psychological stability.

The seasoned negotiator's mindset is not about suppressing emotion. It is about mastering interpretation. It is not about avoiding conflict. It is about navigating it without losing orientation. Anyone can negotiate when stakes are low and time is abundant. The seasoned negotiator reveals themselves when stakes are high and ambiguity is thick. They do not think faster. They think clearer. And, clarity under pressure is the rarest advantage of all.

INSIGHT 60 – EMOTIONAL REGULATION AS PROFESSIONAL SKILL

There is a myth in negotiation that professionalism means detachment. The seasoned negotiator knows better. Professionalism is not the absence of emotion; it is the disciplined management of it.

On a job-site, in a boardroom, across a bargaining table, emotion is always present. Deadlines compress. Money tightens. Pride surfaces. Identity feels exposed. The question is never whether emotion will enter the negotiation. The question is who will regulate it.

The experienced professional understands that emotional regulation is not a personality trait. It is a skill. And like any skill, it can be practiced, refined, and mastered.

The Principle

Your nervous system is part of the negotiation.

Negotiation is cognitive, but it is also physiological.

When a superintendent feels he has been blindsided in a coordination meeting, his heart rate rises. When a labor representative hears language that threatens a member's security, her breathing shortens. When an executive senses loss of authority, his tone sharpens before his words do.

These reactions happen before strategy. The seasoned negotiator recognizes a foundational truth: you cannot think strategically if your nervous system is in fight-or-flight. Emotional flooding narrows perception. It turns complex issues into simple threats. It pushes you toward rigid positions and away from creative solutions.

Regulation is therefore not self-help; it is strategic necessity.

Emotional regulation means:

- Noticing your reaction before it governs your response.
- Creating space between stimulus and reply.
- Choosing language that advances purpose rather than vents pressure.

This does not mean suppressing emotion. Suppression leaks. It shows up in sarcasm, sharp questions, or subtle escalation. Regulation means acknowledging emotion internally while remaining deliberate externally.

The professional asks internally, "What am I reacting to? Loss? Disrespect? Risk?" That moment of awareness restores choice. And choice restores leverage. The party who regulates emotion best often shapes the tone, pace, and trajectory of the negotiation.

The Pitfall

Mistaking intensity for strength.

One of the most common mistakes in high-stakes negotiation is confusing emotional intensity with authority. Raised voices feel powerful. Firm ultimatums feel decisive. Visible frustration can look like commitment. But intensity often signals loss of control. When negotiators react emotionally, several predictable consequences follow:

- They personalize structural problems.
- They escalate language unnecessarily.
- They reduce room for concession.
- They invite reciprocal escalation.

On a job-site, a project manager publicly challenges a subcontractor's competence. The subcontractor responds defensively. The room polarizes. What began as a scheduling issue becomes an identity conflict. The original problem, coordination, gets buried beneath ego and pride.

Another subtle version of this pitfall is internal suppression followed by sudden eruption. Professionals who "keep it together" without processing pressure eventually snap, often at the worst possible moment. A carefully built relationship can erode in a single uncontrolled exchange. The seasoned negotiator understands something counterintuitive:

Calm is not weakness. Calm is command.

Emotional steadiness communicates that you are not threatened, not rushed, not reactive. It projects capacity. And capacity builds credibility. The negotiator who remains composed under pressure often becomes the gravitational center of the room. Others begin orienting to that steadiness.

In contrast, the negotiator who loses regulation forfeits influence—even if their substantive position is strong.

The Pointer

Slow the moment down.

Emotional regulation does not require complex techniques. It requires disciplined micro-practices applied consistently. First, name internally what is happening. "I feel dismissed." "This feels like loss." "That comment triggered defensiveness." Labeling emotion reduces its intensity. It shifts the brain from reaction to analysis.

Second, regulate physically before responding verbally. Lower your breathing. Unclench your jaw. Slow your speech rate. Lean back slightly. These are not cosmetic gestures - they signal safety to your own nervous system. A slower voice changes the entire temperature of a conversation.

Third, reframe before you reply. Instead of, "That's not accurate." Try, "Help me understand how you're seeing that." Instead of, "We can't accept that." Try, "Here's what makes that difficult on our side." Reframing does not concede substance. It preserves stability.

Fourth, use structured pauses. Silence is regulation's ally. A three-second pause feels long in a tense exchange, but it prevents three weeks of damage.

Fifth, separate identity from issue. When emotion spikes, ask, "Is this about the problem - or about how I feel about the problem?"

Seasoned negotiators routinely negotiate difficult issues without negotiating their self-worth. Finally, when appropriate, acknowledge emotion without amplifying it. "This conversation matters to all of us." Or "There's clearly pressure here." Naming shared pressure often diffuses private escalation.

Here is what experienced professionals learn over time: regulation spreads. When one party lowers their tone, others often follow. When one party listens without interruption, defensiveness softens. When one party refuses to escalate, the cycle weakens.

The negotiator who regulates emotion becomes an anchor. This does not mean they never feel frustration, anger, or urgency. It means they do not allow those feelings to dictate behavior.

They understand that reputation is cumulative. Word travels quickly in construction circles, executive networks, and labor communities. People remember who kept composure under strain and who did not. Over time, emotional steadiness becomes part of professional identity. And identity becomes leverage.

Emotional regulation is not softness. It is disciplined restraint in service of long-term influence. In high-stakes environments, technical competence is expected. Strategic thinking is respected. But emotional regulation differentiates. It allows you to:

- Hear information others miss.
- Preserve relationships under pressure.
- Maintain flexibility when others lock in.
- Protect credibility in volatile moments.

The negotiation is rarely decided by the most forceful voice. It is often shaped by the most stable presence. In the end, emotional regulation is not about being calm for its own sake. It is about staying effective when it matters most. And that is the mark of a true professional.

INSIGHT 61 – BUILDING CREDIBILITY OVER TIME

Credibility in negotiation is rarely established in a single moment. It is built gradually, often quietly, through a pattern of consistent behavior observed over time. Experienced negotiators understand that credibility is not something you declare; it is

something others conclude. Every interaction, formal or informal, contributes to that conclusion. The way you communicate, the promises you keep, the way you handle pressure, and the respect you show to others all accumulate into a reputation that precedes you long before a negotiation ever begins.

In many professional environments, particularly those where relationships continue across projects or decisions, credibility functions as a form of currency. When people believe that your words are reliable, that your commitments will be honored, and that your motives are professional rather than manipulative, negotiations become more efficient and less defensive. Parties spend less time questioning intent and more time addressing substance.

In negotiation, especially in high-stakes environments like construction, labor relations, or executive leadership, credibility is the quiet currency that determines whether your words carry weight or evaporate on contact. It is built slowly, tested constantly, and lost quickly.

The Principle

Credibility is the compound interest of consistency.

Credibility grows when your behavior aligns with your words, repeatedly, predictably, and under pressure. It is not about charisma. It is not about having the best argument in the room. It is about reliability across time.

Every interaction deposits or withdraws from your credibility account:

- Do you say what you mean?
- Do you follow through when it costs you something?
- Do you acknowledge constraints honestly?
- Do you correct errors quickly?

People are constantly asking themselves three silent questions about you:

1. Are you competent?
2. Are you honest?
3. Are you predictable under stress?

That third question matters most. Anyone can appear reasonable when stakes are low. Credibility is forged when timelines slip, costs rise, emotions spike, and scrutiny intensifies. If your tone changes with pressure, if your commitments shift when convenient, or if your standards apply selectively, credibility erodes, quietly but decisively.

Over time, consistent behavior builds trust capital. And that capital changes negotiations before they even begin. When you have credibility:

- Your explanations are believed.
- Your constraints are respected.
- Your warnings are taken seriously.
- Your concessions are valued. When you lack credibility:
- Every statement is questioned.

- Every move is scrutinized.
- Every offer is discounted.

Credibility compresses negotiation time. It reduces friction. It lowers defensive posturing. It increases the probability that others will take risks with you. But credibility is cumulative. It is not built in a single dramatic moment. It is built in small, disciplined ones.

The Pitfall

Trying to win the moment instead of protecting the pattern.

The most common credibility failure is short-term opportunism.

Under pressure, negotiators sometimes:

- Overpromise to calm tension.
- Hide constraints to gain leverage.
- Make commitments they hope to renegotiate later.
- Shift positions without explanation.
- Spin partial truths as complete narratives.

These moves may produce a short-term advantage. They may "win" a meeting. But they damage the long-term pattern. Credibility is not destroyed by disagreement. It is destroyed by inconsistency and surprise. When people discover that your words stretch depending on convenience, they begin building defensive structures around you:

- More documentation.
- More oversight.
- Less flexibility.
- Slower decisions.
- Tighter controls.

You don't just lose trust; you increase transaction costs.

Another common pitfall is mistaking likability for

credibility. You can be personable, warm, even charming, and still be seen as unreliable. Conversely, you can be direct, reserved, even tough, and be deeply credible if your behavior is consistent and transparent.

Credibility is not about being liked. It is about being counted on.

There is also a subtle danger in emotional reactivity. If your tone escalates when challenged, if your posture hardens when questioned, or if your commitments fluctuate when you feel threatened, others will experience you as unstable under pressure. And instability erodes credibility faster than disagreement.

The seasoned negotiator resists the temptation to trade long-term credibility for short-term advantage. They understand that patterns outlive moments.

The Pointer

Make small promises and keep them - especially when it hurts.

If credibility compounds, then the strategy is simple, protect the pattern. Here are three practical disciplines to build credibility over time:

1. Narrow Your Commitments. Do not promise what you cannot control. Instead of saying, "We'll have this resolved by Friday," say, "By Friday, we will provide a detailed update and next steps." Precision protects credibility. Overcommitment erodes it. Under-promise slightly. Deliver fully.
2. Surface Constraints Early. When you hide limitations, you create future disappointment. When you disclose them early, you create predictability. Statements like:
   - "Here's where we're constrained."
   - "This part we can move. That part we cannot."

- "If this changes, it affects cost and timeline."

These are credibility builders. They demonstrate clarity and foresight. Surprises damage trust. Transparency stabilizes it.

3. Honor Difficult Commitments Publicly. The most powerful credibility deposits happen when keeping your word cost you something. When you:
   - Absorb responsibility instead of deflecting it.
   - Acknowledge an oversight without excuses.
   - Deliver on an agreement despite internal pressure not to. People notice. Especially constituents and especially opponents.

Credibility does not mean rigidity. You can change positions. You can renegotiate terms. You can adapt to new data. But when you do, explain it. "Based on new information, our position is evolving. Here's why." Consistency does not mean never adjusting. It means adjusting transparently. Building credibility over time requires a long horizon.

You will lose some tactical advantages. You will occasionally concede leverage. You will sometimes say, "We can't do that," when others want you to stretch. But the return is exponential. Over time, you become the person whose word simplifies decisions. The person whose presence reduces volatility. The person others consult before conflict escalates.

And in complex negotiations, especially in industries where relationships repeat and reputations travel, credibility is not just an asset. It is infrastructure.

The seasoned negotiator knows: You are always negotiating your reputation. Every conversation counts. Every commitment leaves a mark.

Protect the pattern. Because in the end, credibility is not

what you say about yourself. It is what time proves about you.

INSIGHT 62 – THE VALUE OF TEACHING NEGOTIATION TO FIELD LEADERS

Construction companies invest heavily in equipment, software, scheduling systems, and safety programs. Yet the single most underdeveloped asset on most projects is the negotiation skill of field leaders. Superintendents, foremen, and project managers

negotiate every day, whether they call it that or not. They negotiate with subcontractors over sequencing, with inspectors over interpretations, with crews over overtime, and with owners over access and expectations.

Most field leaders were promoted for technical competence. Few were trained for negotiation competence. That gap is expensive.

Teaching negotiation to field leaders changes the culture and profitability of an organization.

The Principle

Negotiation is already happening at the edge.

Negotiation does not begin in the boardroom. It begins on the jobsite. Every time a superintendent says, "We need you to adjust your manpower," or a foreman says, "We can't hit that date without access," a negotiation is unfolding. It may be informal. It may be unrecognized. But it is shaping cost, schedule, morale, and risk in real time.

Field leaders operate at the point of friction, where plans meet reality, drawings are interpreted, delays ripple outward, and ambiguities surface. Personalities clash, and decisions must be made under pressure.

When field leaders lack negotiation training, three things typically happen:

1. Issues escalate upward unnecessarily.
2. Positions harden prematurely.
3. Relationships deteriorate under stress.

Executives often assume negotiation is a strategic skill reserved for senior leadership. In truth, it is an operational skill required at the edge of execution.

When field leaders understand negotiation principles, separating positions from interests, managing emotion, sequencing issues, and preserving optionality they stop reacting and start structuring conversations. They recognize that a schedule dispute may really be about manpower risk. That resistance may be about saving face, and that a demand may be masking fear.

Teaching negotiation to field leaders is not about making them "softer." It is about making them more effective under pressure. It reduces friction before it compounds.

The Pitfall

Promoting technicians without equipping them.

The most common mistake organizations make is assuming experience equals negotiation competence. A field leader who has survived twenty projects may feel confident. But survival is not the same as mastery. Experience without reflection can entrench bad habits such as:

- Arguing louder when challenged.
- Escalating quickly to contract language.
- Using authority instead of inquiry.
- Treating every disagreement as a win-lose contest.

These habits may "work" short term. They may secure compliance. But they quietly increase long-term costs, change orders driven by distrust, subcontractors pricing in risk premiums, crews disengaging under rigid management.

Another mistake is offering negotiation training only to executives. The irony is stark: executives negotiate a handful of major contracts each year. Field leaders negotiate dozens of micro-conflicts every week.

If negotiation is only taught at the top, the organization remains reactive at the bottom.

Worse, untrained field leaders can unintentionally undermine senior negotiations. A careless email. A heated exchange. A public ultimatum. These moments shape perceptions long before formal talks begin.

Without training, field leaders often believe that strength equals inflexibility. They fear appearing weak if they ask questions. They confuse concession with collapse. So, they double down on positions when what is needed is structured curiosity.

The pitfall is not incompetence. It is underinvestment in relational skill at the very level where relationships matter most.

The Pointer

Equip the edge, not just the executive suite.

Teaching negotiation to field leaders requires a shift in mindset: treat negotiation as an operational discipline, not an executive art. Start with practical frameworks:

- Identify the real issue before debating solutions.
- Distinguish emotion from substance.
- Sequence conversations—don't tackle everything at once.
- Name tension without escalating it.
- Preserve dignity while protecting standards.

Field leaders do not need academic theory. They need field-ready tools. For example:

- Instead of saying, "That's not in our scope," teach them to say, "Help me understand what outcome you're trying to protect here."
- Instead of responding to escalation with escalation, teach them to pause and reframe: "It sounds like schedule risk is the real concern. Let's look at that together."

These small adjustments change trajectories. Organizations that train field leaders in negotiation report:

- Fewer disputes reaching formal claims.
- Faster issue resolution.
- Stronger subcontractor partnerships.
- Higher crew morale.
- Reduced leadership burnout.

There is another benefit rarely discussed and that is credibility. When field leaders negotiate thoughtfully, they project steadiness. Subcontractors feel heard. Inspectors feel respected. Owners feel informed rather than surprised. That credibility compounds across projects.

Training field leaders also aligns language across the organization. When everyone understands the difference between positions and interests, or the danger of reactive escalation, internal conversations become more strategic. The culture shifts from blame to problem-solving.

Finally, negotiation training protects leadership energy. Field leaders operate in relentless environments. Every unresolved conflict drains attention. Teaching them structured negotiation reduces cognitive noise. It gives them a way to approach friction without absorbing it emotionally. They stop taking every challenge personally. They start seeing patterns.

When negotiation is taught at the field level, the organization becomes more resilient. Problems are addressed earlier. Conversations are clearer. Emotions are managed rather than mirrored. Authority is used strategically rather than reflexively.

Executives often ask, "What is the ROI of negotiation training?" The answer is visible in fewer claims, smoother schedules, stronger reputations, and lower turnover. But it is also visible in something less measurable: confidence under pressure. A trained field leader does not fear disagreement. He or she expects it, and knows how to work through it.

Negotiation is not a special event reserved for contract signings. It is the daily discipline of aligning interests in an imperfect environment. Teach it where friction lives. Teach it at the edge.

When field leaders negotiate well, projects stabilize, relationships strengthen, and the entire organization performs at a higher level.

INSIGHT 63 – CONSENSUS VS. COMMAND DECISION

Leadership in negotiation is not simply about influence across the table. It is also about clarity behind it. The most damaging mistakes in complex environments do not happen because someone argued poorly with the other side. They happen because

the team on one side never decided how decisions would actually be made.

In high-stakes environments, leaders often drift between consensus and command without ever naming which one they are using. The confusion that follows is predictable: delays, quiet resentment, passive resistance, or sudden overruling.

The seasoned negotiator understands that consensus and command are not moral opposites. They are tools. And like all tools, they must be used deliberately.

The Principle

Match the decision mode to the risk and the responsibility.

Consensus is powerful. It builds commitment, surfaces blind spots, and strengthens relationships. When people help shape a decision, they defend it. They carry it. They own it.

Command decisions are also powerful. They create speed, clarity, and accountability. When time is short or responsibility is singular, someone must decide—and everyone must know who that someone is. The principle is simple: Use consensus to build alignment when commitment is essential. Use command when clarity and speed outweigh broad input. Consensus works best when:

- The issue affects multiple stakeholders long-term.
- Implementation requires cooperation across roles.
- The cost of misalignment is higher than the cost of delay. Command works best when:
- Time pressure is real.
- Accountability sits clearly with one role.
- The risk of indecision exceeds the risk of imperfection.

The seasoned negotiator makes the decision mode explicit. Before the discussion begins, they say, "We are gathering input, and I will decide." Or, "We will not move forward until we reach agreement." Clarity about process reduces anxiety. People can tolerate outcomes they dislike far more easily than processes they don't understand.

The Pitfall

Mistaking consensus for harmony and command for strength.

The first pitfall is the illusion of consensus. Leaders say, "Is everyone good with this?" Silence follows. The leader interprets silence as agreement. It is not agreement. It is risk management. People stay quiet to avoid conflict, not because they are aligned.

False consensus produces weak commitment. Weeks later, implementation falters. Stakeholders drag their feet. Someone says, "I had concerns from the beginning." The leader feels betrayed. But the betrayal happened earlier—when dissent was never invited.

The second pitfall is overusing command as a demonstration of strength. Some leaders equate decisiveness with authority. They make unilateral calls in situations that require shared ownership. The short-term result is efficiency. The long-term result is erosion of trust.

In negotiation settings, this mistake is amplified. A leader may negotiate externally in a collaborative spirit while ruling internally by decree. The team senses the inconsistency. Credibility weakens. Internal fractures show up across the table.

Another subtle danger is what might be called "pseudo-consensus." The group debates extensively, but everyone knows the decision-maker has already decided. The discussion becomes theater. Participants learn that input is performative, not influential.

Over time, people stop offering insight. They conserve energy.

And the organization loses its collective intelligence.

The Pointer

Declare the decision rule before the debate.

The most practical pointer is this: State the decision rule before you invite discussion. Try language like:

- "We are in consultation mode. I will make the final call after hearing your perspectives."
- "This requires full buy-in. If we cannot align, we will keep working."
- "We need rapid direction. I'm deciding today, but I want two key risks from each of you before I do."

This single act changes the emotional climate. When people know whether they are influencing or deciding, they calibrate their energy accordingly.

Second, separate input from authority. Invite disagreement explicitly:

- "What am I missing?"
- "If this fails, what will be the reason?"
- "Who sees this differently?"

Silence should never be accepted as consensus. Draw it out. The quietest voice may hold the most valuable insight.

Third, own the weight of command decisions. If you must decide unilaterally, do so cleanly. Avoid softening it with phrases like "We all agree..." when you know that isn't true. Instead say, "I've heard the concerns. Given the time constraints, I'm deciding to proceed. If new information emerges, we'll revisit." This communicates strength without pretending unanimity.

Finally, understand that consensus is about commitment, not unanimity. Total agreement is rare. What matters is whether stakeholders can support the decision publicly, even if it was not their first choice. The seasoned negotiator asks a crucial follow-up question, "Can you support this decision going forward?" That question measures alignment more accurately than "Does everyone agree?"

In complex negotiations, especially in environments like construction, labor relations, or executive leadership, how you decide internally affects how you negotiate externally. If your team is unclear about authority, the other side will sense hesitation. If your team feels ignored, they will undercut implementation. If your team is aligned, even imperfectly, your external posture strengthens. Consensus builds resilience. Command builds velocity.

The skilled leader knows when to slow down and when to step forward. They do not confuse participation with weakness or decisiveness with dominance. They recognize that both modes serve a larger goal: sustainable outcomes.

In the end, the question is not whether consensus or command is superior. The question is whether you chose deliberately. And, whether the people who must carry the decision understand how it was made, and why.

INSIGHT 64 – STRATEGIC PATIENCE

In high-stakes negotiation, the pressure to move is constant. Deadlines loom. Constituents demand updates. Silence feels dangerous. Momentum feels productive. And yet, some of the most consequential errors in negotiation happen not because someone

moved too slowly, but because they moved too quickly.

Strategic patience is not passive waiting. It is disciplined timing. It is the decision to delay reaction in order to increase leverage, clarity, and advantage. The seasoned negotiator understands that timing is not incidental to strategy. It is strategy.

The Principle

Time is a source of leverage.

Most negotiators treat time as an external constraint; something imposed on them. Strategic patience reframes time as an asset to be managed. Time does three powerful things in negotiation:

1. It reveals information. When you resist the urge to fill silence or rush to closure, the other side often discloses more than they intended. Deadlines clarify who actually has pressure. Silence exposes uncertainty.
2. It cools emotion. Heated exchanges rarely produce durable agreements. Pauses allow identity threats and perceived losses to settle. When emotions settle, cognition returns.
3. It shifts bargaining power. The party who appears least rushed often gains psychological leverage. Urgency signals need. Patience signals optionality.

Strategic patience is not stalling for its own sake. It is deliberate pacing aligned with objectives. The seasoned negotiator knows when to accelerate and when to slow the tempo. They understand that speed is a tactic, but timing is a discipline.

On complex projects, particularly in construction, labor relations, or multi-party agreements, rushed decisions often create downstream costs that far exceed the discomfort of delay. The negotiator who can tolerate temporary ambiguity often secures longer-term stability. Control your reaction to time, and you control more of the negotiation than you think.

The Pitfall

Mistaking motion for progress.

The greatest enemy of strategic patience is anxiety. Negotiators feel pressure to:

- "Keep things moving."
- Avoid awkward silence.
- Demonstrate responsiveness.
- Show decisiveness.

This pressure leads to premature concessions, over-explaining positions, or accepting terms before fully understanding implications.

Silence feels like weakness. Delay feels like incompetence. Reflection feels like indecision. So, people fill the space. They respond immediately to proposals. They negotiate against themselves when the other side says nothing. They shorten their own deadlines. They interpret pause as rejection rather than recalibration. In doing so, they give away leverage.

Another common mistake is artificial urgency. A party announces, "This offer expires at 5 p.m." The inexperienced negotiator reacts as if the clock is real and immovable. The seasoned negotiator asks, "Who benefits from this deadline? What happens if it passes?"

Not all deadlines are equal. Some are operational realities. Others are strategic pressure tactics. The pitfall is confusing urgency with importance. Important decisions often require patience. Urgent demands often mask insecurity.

Finally, there is the internal rush. Leaders sometimes push for closure because unresolved issues create discomfort. Ambiguity is psychologically taxing. But agreements made to relieve discomfort rarely hold under stress.

Strategic impatience produces fragile outcomes.

The Pointer

Slow the tempo without losing momentum.

Strategic patience is not about freezing the process. It is about controlling tempo while maintaining direction. Here are three practical ways to apply it:

1. Use Structured Pauses - When proposals shift the landscape, resist immediate response. Instead say:
   - "Let's take time to review this carefully."
   - "We need to evaluate implications before reacting."
   - "We'll respond tomorrow."

Structured pauses signal seriousness, not avoidance. They protect you from reactive decisions and allow your team to analyze second and third order effects.

In high-stakes environments, even a 24-hour delay can significantly improve clarity.

2. Separate Decision from Discussion. Not every conversation requires an immediate decision.

Seasoned negotiators are explicit:

- "We're discussing today. We're not deciding today."
- "Let's surface all issues before we close any."

This keeps momentum without forcing premature commitment. It allows exploration without locking into positions. It also prevents one side from exploiting momentum to force partial agreements that weaken overall leverage.

3. Test Deadlines. When confronted with urgency, calmly test it:

- “Help me understand what happens if we don’t resolve this today.”
- “Is that a hard-operational deadline or a preference?”
- “What flexibility exists?”

This is not confrontation. It is clarification. Often, deadlines soften under inquiry. And if they do not, you now understand the real constraint and can negotiate within reality instead of assumption.

Strategic patience requires emotional regulation. You must manage your own discomfort with silence, ambiguity, and external pressure. In tense negotiations, silence can feel like exposure. Waiting can feel like loss of control. But often, waiting is control.

The seasoned negotiator understands that:

- The first proposal is rarely the final one.
- The first emotional reaction is rarely the most accurate one.
- The first deadline is rarely the only one.

Patience also signals confidence. When you are not scrambling, over-explaining, or rushing to agreement, you project stability. Stability attracts concessions.

In labor negotiations, job-site disputes, executive decision-making, and complex contracts, patience prevents escalation. Many conflicts intensify not because of substantive disagreement but because someone reacted too quickly to perceived disrespect or threat. A well-timed pause can prevent weeks of damage.

This chapter is not an argument for delay as a universal tactic. Excessive delay can erode trust and signal bad faith. Strategic patience must be paired with transparency and progress. The difference lies in intent. Passive delay avoids decision. Strategic patience prepares for better decision.

Passive delay hides. Strategic patience clarifies. Passive delay weakens credibility. Strategic patience strengthens leverage.

In negotiation, timing communicates as much as words. When you control your tempo, you influence theirs. And in high-stakes environments, the negotiator who masters time often masters the table.

Strategic patience is not about waiting longer.

INSIGHT 65 – KNOWING WHEN TO ESCALATE

There is a moment in difficult negotiations when the question shifts from how do I solve this to should this be solved here? Escalation is not surrender. It is not failure. And it is not weakness. It is a strategic decision about level, authority, and consequence.

Many negotiations stall not because the problem is unsolvable, but because it is being handled at the wrong altitude. Field leaders try to resolve issues that require executive authority. Executives wade into operational disputes that should remain local. Emotions rise. Positions harden, and trust erodes.

Knowing when to escalate is not about passing the problem upward. It is about recognizing when resolution requires a different forum, a broader mandate, or higher consequence alignment. The seasoned negotiator understands that escalation is a tool—not a threat.

The Principle

Escalate when authority, risk, or identity exceed the table.

Escalation becomes appropriate when one of three thresholds has been crossed:

1. Authority - The parties at the table do not have the power to authorize the necessary trade-offs.
2. Risk - The consequences now exceed the level at which the decision is being made.
3. Identity - The issue has become symbolic, reputational, or precedent-setting beyond the negotiators' scope.

Most failed negotiations continue too long at a level that lacks authority. People argue over concessions they cannot approve. They debate options they are not empowered to grant. They imply flexibility they cannot deliver. This creates false movement. It feels like negotiation, but it is performance. A seasoned negotiator asks early, who actually owns this decision, whose risk tolerance is implicated, and what precedent might this set?

When the answers point upward, escalation is not dramatic. It is disciplined.

But escalation is not only vertical. Sometimes it is lateral, bringing in legal, finance, risk management, or executive sponsors. Sometimes it is structural, changing the forum, separating issues, or formalizing the discussion.

Escalation is not about raising voices. It is about raising altitude.

And timing matters.

Escalate too early and you signal incapacity. Escalate too late and damage hardens. The art lies in recognizing when continued discussion at the current level will produce diminishing returns, or worse, entrenched resistance. If you feel repetition without progress, if authority gaps are obvious, or if the issue has become symbolic beyond scope, you are likely at the escalation threshold.

The question is no longer can we solve it? It is are we the right ones to solve it?

The Pitfall

Treating escalation as either failure or weapon.

There are two common errors. The first is refusing to escalate out of pride. Leaders cling to ownership. They believe taking something upward signals incompetence. They fear being perceived as unable to "handle their business." So, they push harder. They argue longer. They exhaust goodwill. What began as a manageable disagreement becomes personal. By the time it reaches higher authority, it is loaded with resentment.

The second error is weaponizing escalation. Some negotiators escalate prematurely to apply pressure. They "go over someone's head" to force compliance. They bypass process to intimidate. They use hierarchy as leverage instead of structure. This rarely ends well. Weaponized escalation creates defensiveness, erodes relationships, and turns solvable problems into political battles. Even if it produces short-term compliance, it damages long-term trust.

Escalation should clarify responsibility - not create humiliation.

Another subtle pitfall is escalating emotion rather than structure. People say they are escalating the issue, but what they escalate is tone. Emails get sharper. Meetings get larger. Language gets more formal and accusatory. That is not escalation. That is amplification.

True escalation increases decision authority and alignment—not noise. The seasoned negotiator distinguishes between:

- Escalating to resolve.
- Escalating to win.
- Escalating to vent. Only the first is strategic.

The Pointer

Escalate with framing, not friction.

If escalation becomes necessary, how you frame it determines whether it builds resolution or resistance. First, make the authority gap explicit without blame. "I don't believe either of us has the mandate to authorize this level of risk. Let's involve those who do." This reframes escalation as structural necessity, not personal failure.

Second, protect the relationship at your level. Escalation should never feel like betrayal. It should feel like alignment. Signal clearly: "This isn't about going around you. It's about ensuring the right decision-makers weigh in."

Third, escalate jointly whenever possible. Inviting the other party into the escalation process reduces defensiveness. It shifts the posture from adversarial to collaborative. "Let's take this upward together."

Fourth, define the purpose of escalation. Are you seeking policy clarification? Budget authority? Risk tolerance alignment? Executive endorsement? Undefined escalation creates chaos. Defined escalation creates clarity.

Finally, reset tone at the higher level. Escalation should not carry accumulated frustration into the new forum. It should elevate perspective. Frame the issue as a shared challenge, not a battle summary. A seasoned negotiator prepares upward briefings carefully:

- Clear issue definition.
- Impact if unresolved.
- Options considered.
- Authority required.

Escalation done well demonstrates professionalism, not incapacity. And sometimes, escalation itself changes behavior. When parties know that unresolved matters will move upward, incentives shift. Responsibility sharpens. Posturing decreases. Escalation should never be a threat. It should be a governance mechanism.

Negotiation is often described as movement toward agreement. Less often is it described as movement across levels. The wisdom lies in recognizing when persistence becomes counterproductive and when perspective must widen. Escalation is not about surrendering control. It is about placing the issue where it can actually be resolved. Stay too low, and you suffocate progress. Go too high, and you waste authority.

The seasoned negotiator watches for thresholds, authority, risk, identity, and acts deliberately. Knowing when to escalate is not dramatic. It is disciplined. And discipline, not ego, is what keeps negotiation professional.

INSIGHT 66 – KNOWING WHEN TO DE-ESCALATE

In negotiation and conflict, escalation gets the headlines. People remember the blow-ups, the ultimatums, the walk-outs. But seasoned professionals understand something quieter and far more powerful - knowing when to de-escalate.

De-escalation is not surrender. It is not weakness. It is disciplined control of temperature. It is the ability to slow momentum before damage compounds.

On a job-site, in a boardroom, or across a bargaining table, the difference between professionals and amateurs often shows up in this single decision, do we push harder - or do we lower the heat?

Let's examine the principle behind de-escalation, the common pitfall that prevents it, and the pointer that separates reactive leaders from strategic ones.

The Principle

Temperature drives judgment.

Conflict has a temperature. Voices rise. Language sharpens. Positions harden. Deadlines get weaponized. Identity creeps in. Once the emotional temperature climbs high enough, reasoning narrows. People stop processing nuance and begin defending territory.

Escalation narrows options. De-escalation reopens them.

The seasoned negotiator understands that high emotion compresses thinking. When someone feels attacked, disrespected, or cornered, their nervous system shifts into defense mode. In that state, persuasion becomes nearly impossible. Every argument will sound like pressure. Every clarification sounds like criticism.

De-escalation is the intentional lowering of emotional temperature so rational thinking can return. It may mean pausing the meeting. It may mean softening tone. It may mean acknowledging impact before debating facts or it may mean separating people from the issue.

Lowering the heat does not mean lowering standards. It means creating conditions where standards can be discussed without combustion.

In complex negotiations, the most expensive mistakes are rarely caused by bad logic. They are caused by overheated judgment. The professional knows, if the temperature is too high, nothing productive will stick.

The Pitfall

Mistaking intensity for strength.

Many leaders escalate because they equate intensity with strength. They believe:

- If I push harder, they'll back down.
- If I show no emotion, I'll appear strong.
- If I concede tone, I concede ground.
- If I pause, I lose leverage.

This is the trap. Escalation can feel powerful in the moment. It signals dominance. It satisfies ego. It reassures constituents that you are "standing firm." But intensity often invites equal or greater intensity in return. Conflict spirals.

The mistake is assuming that backing off emotionally equals backing off substantively. It does not. You can de-escalate tone while holding your position. You can validate emotion without validating accusation. You can slow momentum without surrendering leverage.

Another version of this pitfall is the fear of appearing weak. In many professional cultures, particularly male-dominated or performance-driven environments, calm is misread as softness. So, leaders escalate to pro-protect identity.

Ironically, uncontrolled escalation signals the opposite of strength. It reveals that emotion is driving strategy. When escalation becomes reciprocal, the conversation shifts from problem-solving to reputation management. Now both sides are protecting pride rather than protecting outcomes. That is when damage compounds. The amateur asks, "How do I win this exchange?" The seasoned negotiator asks, "What happens if this keeps heating up?"

The Pointer

Control the pace before you control the outcome.

De-escalation is rarely dramatic. It is procedural. Here is what it looks like in practice:

1. Name the temperature without accusation. "I think we're getting heated. Let's slow this down." This signals awareness without blame. It interrupts the spiral.
2. Shift from position to impact. Instead of arguing facts, acknowledge effect. "I hear that this feels like we changed the deal." You are not conceding fault. You are addressing emotional data.
3. Slow the clock. Escalation feeds on urgency. Introduce space. "Let's take ten minutes." "Let's come back to this tomorrow morning." Time cools what pressure inflames.
4. Lower your own volume first. Emotional contagion is real. Calm is contagious too. Speak slower. Soften tone. Maintain posture. You cannot lower the room's temperature while raising your own.
5. Separate the audience from the problem. Escalation intensifies when constituencies are watching. If possible, move the hardest conversations offline. People compromise more rationally without spectators.
6. Re-anchor purpose. "Both of us need this project to finish on time." Shared objectives reduce zero-sum thinking. The seasoned negotiator understands timing. Not every moment calls for pressure. Not every push produces movement. Sometimes movement only becomes possible after heat dissipates. De-escalation preserves options. Escalation consumes them.

There are moments when escalation is necessary, when safety, legality, or ethical boundaries are at risk. But most professional conflict does not begin there. It escalates there. The critical skill is discernment. Ask yourself:

- Is the issue substantive—or emotional?
- Are we solving a problem—or protecting ego?
- Is pressure increasing clarity—or narrowing thinking?
- Will pushing now improve the outcome—or damage the relationship?

If emotion is outpacing substance, it is time to de-escalate. The true mark of authority is not how loudly you can press your case. It is how steadily you can control the temperature of the room.

When you master de-escalation, you gain something far more powerful than dominance. You gain influence. When others lose control and you do not, you become the stabilizing force. And in high-stakes negotiations, the person who stabilizes the room often shapes the outcome. De-escalation is not retreat. It is strategic restraint. And knowing when to apply it may be one of the most professional skills you ever develop.

INSIGHT 67 – INSTITUTIONAL MEMORY AND REPUTATION

In negotiation, nothing begins at zero. Every conversation enters a room already occupied - by history, by stories, by remembered slights, by prior concessions, and by patterns of behavior. Even when the faces change, the memory remains.

Institutional memory and reputation are invisible participants at the table. They influence expectations before the first word is spoken. They shape whether trust is extended cautiously - or not at all. The seasoned negotiator understands this reality. The inexperienced one ignores it at their peril.

Here, we examine the principle behind institutional memory, the pitfall of mismanaging reputation, and the pointer that distinguishes professionals from amateurs.

The Principle

The organization negotiates long before you do.

Institutional memory is the collective memory of how your organization has behaved in the past. It includes formal agreements, informal promises, tone, timing, and patterns. Reputation is the external summary of that memory.

People rarely negotiate only with you. They negotiate with what they believe about your organization. If your firm has a pattern of reopening settled issues, others come armed for trench warfare. If you consistently deliver on commitments, even small ones, your counterparts arrive more open. If your leadership punishes compromise internally, external parties will expect rigidity.

Institutional memory lives in meeting minutes, grievance files, email chains, jobsite stories, and union halls. It lives in hallway conversations that begin with, "Last time they said…" It survives leadership turnover. It outlives strategy shifts. It is sticky.

Reputation is memory distilled. The seasoned negotiator respects this gravity. They prepare not just for the substance of the issue, but for the historical context surrounding it. They ask:

- What happened the last three times this issue arose?
- Who still remembers it?
- What narrative has formed about our behavior?
- Where do we carry trust—and where do we carry doubt?

Negotiation is cumulative. You are always negotiating the next deal while closing the current one. Your reputation compounds, positively or negatively, with every interaction.

The Pitfall

Treating each negotiation as isolated.

The most common mistake is assuming every negotiation is a fresh start. Leaders say, "That was before my time," as if memory resets with a new badge or title.

It does not. Institutional memory does not respond to disclaimers.

When leaders ignore history, they unintentionally reinforce it. If past behavior included aggressive posturing, delayed payments, hidden clauses, or public criticism, counterparts expect recurrence. And when those expectations are not acknowledged, they become defensive in advance.

Another mistake is focusing only on winning the moment. Short-term advantage often creates long-term cost. A tactic that extracts a concession today may erode credibility tomorrow. Overusing leverage, surprising the other side late in the process, or shifting positions without explanation damages the invisible ledger that tracks trust.

There is also the internal dimension. Organizations sometimes suffer from selective memory, remembering only their own concessions while forgetting their rigidity. This self-serving narrative hardens attitudes and blinds leaders to how they are perceived externally.

The danger is cumulative. Once an organization develops a reputation for unpredictability, inflexibility, or opportunism, every negotiation becomes more expensive. Counterparts build in buffers. They document everything. They escalate faster. They demand more up front. The cost of mistrust shows up in time, legal review, contingency pricing, and relational friction.

Reputation is slow to build and quick to fracture. And silence about the past is rarely neutral. It often signals avoidance.

Manage memory deliberately.

The seasoned negotiator does something different. They treat institutional memory as an asset to manage, not a burden to ignore.

First, they surface the history. They say, calmly and directly, "The last time we discussed this, it didn't go well. I'd like to understand what didn't work from your perspective."

This simple acknowledgment lowers defenses. It signals awareness. It demonstrates maturity. It prevents unspoken grievances from steering the conversation from beneath the surface.

Second, they align behavior with declared values. If your organization claims to value partnership, transparency, or fairness, those words must be visible in action, especially under pressure. Reputation is built in difficult moments, not easy ones. Consistency under strain carries more weight than slogans during calm.

Third, they protect small commitments. Large agreements attract attention. Small follow-through builds trust. Returning calls when promised. Delivering documents on time. Clarifying misunderstandings quickly. These behaviors accumulate and institutional memory records them quietly, but reliably.

Fourth, they repair damage proactively. When missteps occur, and they will, the professional addresses them before they calcify into narrative. Acknowledging an error does not weaken reputation; it strengthens credibility. People do not expect perfection. They expect accountability.

Finally, they think beyond the immediate table. Every negotiation sends signals to observers—constituents, internal teams, and future partners. Leaders who manage reputation understand they are modeling standards for their own organization. Institutional memory forms internally as much as externally. If your team observes you honoring commitments even when inconvenient, they adopt the same discipline.

Reputation is not public relations. It is behavioral consistency over time. The seasoned negotiator knows that leverage fluctuates, market conditions change, and leadership rotates. But reputation persists. It is the interest rate applied to every future negotiation. A strong one lowers the cost of agreement. A weak one increases it.

Institutional memory cannot be erased, but it can be reshaped. Every interaction is an opportunity to reinforce a pattern or rewrite one. In the end, negotiation is not only about what you gain today. It is about what others expect from you tomorrow.

And tomorrow's expectations begin forming now. It is disciplined responsibility.

INSIGHT 68 – NEGOTIATION AS STEWARDSHIP

Most people think negotiation is about winning. Seasoned negotiators understand it is about stewardship. Stewardship means you are temporarily entrusted with something that does not belong solely to you, authority, resources, relationships, reputation, and institutional trust. You are not merely closing a deal; you are managing consequences that extend beyond the room and beyond the moment.

When negotiation is framed as conquest, the focus narrows to leverage and outcome. When it is framed as stewardship, the focus expands to responsibility and durability. This distinction changes everything.

The Principle

You are a temporary custodian of long-term interests.

A steward negotiates with the awareness that today's decision shapes tomorrow's landscape. Every concession, every tone, every public statement affects the broader ecosystem in which future negotiations will occur.

You are not only representing your own preferences. You are representing stakeholders who are absent from the room: employees who will live under the agreement, constituents who will judge it, future leaders who will inherit its consequences, and even adversaries who must continue working with you after the headlines fade. Stewardship demands three disciplines.

First, widen the time horizon. Short-term victories that fracture trust often become long-term liabilities. An agreement extracted through humiliation or excessive pressure may be technically successful and strategically disastrous.

Second, protect the institution. A negotiator's behavior becomes part of the institutional memory. If you establish a pattern of fairness and reliability, future talks begin with goodwill. If you establish a pattern of brinkmanship and volatility, every future negotiation begins with suspicion.

Third, preserve relationships as assets. Relationships are not sentimental add-ons; they are infrastructure. They determine the speed and efficiency of future agreements. A steward does not burn infrastructure to power a single outcome.

This is particularly true in industries, governments, and communities where parties negotiate repeatedly. In these environments, negotiation is not an event. It is a cycle. The steward negotiates in a way that strengthens the system, not just the deal.

The Pitfall

Mistaking authority for ownership.

The most common failure in stewardship is ego. Authority feels like ownership. You have the power to sign. You have the title. You have the leverage. It becomes easy to treat the negotiation as a personal proving ground.

This manifests in several ways:

- Driving harder than necessary to demonstrate dominance.
- Refusing reasonable compromises to avoid appearing weak.
- Prioritizing optics over sustainability.
- Framing the negotiation as a battle to be won rather than a responsibility to be managed.

When ego enters the room, stewardship exits.

Another variation of this pitfall is over-identification with the immediate constituency. A negotiator may feel intense pressure from their own side—board members, labor representatives, political supporters, executive leadership. That pressure can create a false urgency to extract maximum visible gain.

But stewardship requires balance. You must protect your constituency without destabilizing the broader system they depend on. Short-term applause from your side can become long-term regret for everyone. The steward resists performative toughness. They understand that symbolic victories often carry hidden costs.

There is also a quieter pitfall, neglect. Some negotiators drift into passive accommodation in the name of harmony. That, too, is a failure of stewardship. You are entrusted with protecting legitimate interests. Avoiding conflict at the expense of those interests is not stewardship; it is abdication. Stewardship is neither aggression nor avoidance. It is disciplined responsibility.

The Pointer

Negotiate as if you will face the consequences personally.

A practical way to operationalize stewardship is to ask three questions before closing any agreement:

- Would I defend this decision publicly a year from now?
- Does this outcome strengthen or weaken future negotiations?
- If roles were reversed, would I view this as fair?

These questions force perspective beyond immediate pressure.

Another powerful pointer is to separate personal pride from institutional protection. When you feel reactive, when your status, competence, or authority feels challenged, pause. Ask yourself whether the reaction protects the institution or merely protects your ego.

Stewards slow down at precisely the moment others speed up. You can also model stewardship explicitly. Articulate it. Say things like:

- "We need an agreement that both sides can live with long term."
- "We'll be working together after this is resolved."
- "Let's make sure this holds up six months from now."

Language shapes norms. When you frame the negotiation as a shared responsibility rather than a contest, you elevate the tone of the room.

Finally, build guardrails into your preparation. Before

negotiations begin, clarify:

- Non-negotiable principles that protect institutional integrity.
- Acceptable trade-offs that preserve relationships.
- Red lines that defend core interests without unnecessary escalation.

Preparation anchored in stewardship reduces the temptation to improvise from emotion. Stewardship does not make negotiation softer. It makes it steadier.

The steward can be firm. They can walk away. They can hold a line. But they do so with clarity about why they are doing it and whom they are protecting.

They understand that power is transient. Titles change. Roles rotate. Markets shift. But reputation compounds.

When people believe you negotiate as a steward, fairly, consistently, and responsibly, they approach you differently. They prepare differently. They escalate less quickly. They trust that even in conflict, you are not reckless. In high-stakes environments, that trust is a strategic advantage.

Negotiation as stewardship is the quiet discipline of thinking beyond yourself. It is the refusal to confuse authority with ownership. It is the commitment to leave the table and the institution stronger than you found it.

The steward does not ask, "Did I win?" The steward asks, "Did I protect what was entrusted to me?"

CONCLUSION: PLAYING THE LONG GAME

Negotiation, in its most practical form, is not an event. It is a professional discipline practiced over time. The conversations that shape outcomes rarely begin at the conference table and they rarely end when the meeting adjourns. They unfold across relationships, reputations, credibility, and the accumulated decisions leaders make long before a formal negotiation ever begins. This is why the seasoned negotiator learns to think in terms of the long game.

The long game recognizes that influence compounds. Every conversation leaves a trace. Every decision signals priorities. Every interaction either strengthens or weakens credibility. Over time, people begin to anticipate how you will behave in difficult situations. They learn whether you escalate conflict unnecessarily, whether you listen before responding, and whether your word holds when pressure increases.

Negotiators who focus only on short-term victories often damage the very relationships that make future agreements possible. A leader who wins aggressively today may find that tomorrow's negotiations begin from a position of skepticism or resistance. In contrast, leaders who demonstrate consistency, fairness, and disciplined judgment accumulate something far more valuable than a single agreement. It's known as trust capital.

Trust capital is the quiet advantage of experienced negotiators. It cannot be demanded and it cannot be manufactured quickly. It is built gradually through reliability, integrity, and thoughtful restraint. Over time, it changes how others approach you. Conversations become more candid. Problems are surfaced earlier. Opposing parties become more willing to explore solutions rather than defend positions.

This is the strategic advantage of the long game. But with influence comes something many negotiators fail to consider carefully enough and that's responsibility.

Influence is not simply the ability to persuade. It is the ability to shape outcomes that affect other people's livelihoods, reputations, and opportunities. Leaders often underestimate how heavily their words carry weight in negotiations. A careless remark can escalate tensions. A poorly timed decision can undermine trust. Conversely, a measured response can stabilize a situation that might otherwise spiral into conflict. Experienced negotiators understand that authority amplifies consequences and the responsibility of influence requires discipline in three areas.

First, it requires emotional discipline. Leaders must regulate their own reactions before attempting to manage the reactions of others. Negotiations often generate frustration, urgency, and pressure. When leaders allow these emotions to dictate their behavior, they unintentionally legitimize the same reactions in others. The result is escalation rather than resolution.

Second, it requires intellectual discipline. Complex negotiations rarely hinge on a single issue. They involve layered interests, organizational pressures, and identity concerns that may not be visible on the surface. Effective negotiators resist the temptation to oversimplify. They ask better questions, consider broader implications, and recognize that solving the wrong problem efficiently still produces the wrong outcome.

Third, it requires ethical discipline. Negotiation offers many opportunities to manipulate information, apply pressure, or exploit temporary advantages. While such tactics may produce immediate gains, they almost always carry long-term costs. The leaders who sustain influence over decades are those who understand that credibility is a strategic asset worth protecting. Influence without responsibility eventually destroys itself.

This brings us to the most important audience for the ideas in this book - future leaders. Many emerging leaders assume negotiation is primarily about techniques, phrases to say, tactics to deploy, or strategies to outmaneuver an opponent. Those tools can be useful, but they are not the foundation of effective negotiation. The real foundation is judgment.

Judgment develops through experience, reflection, and an understanding of human dynamics. It is the ability to recognize when to push forward and when to pause. When to escalate and when to de-escalate. When consensus strengthens a decision and when decisive leadership is required.

Future leaders must also recognize that negotiation happens continuously within organizations, not just between them. Every time priorities are set, resources are allocated, or expectations are clarified, negotiation is occurring. Leaders who ignore this reality often find themselves surprised by resistance that has been building quietly for months.

The most effective leaders do something different. They recognize negotiation as a core leadership capability. They teach it to their teams. They model disciplined communication during disagreement. They treat conflict not as something to avoid but as something to manage constructively.

When leaders approach negotiation this way, organizations change. Conversations become more productive. Problems surface earlier. Decisions improve because more perspectives are considered before positions harden. Perhaps most importantly, people learn that disagreement does not have to destroy relationships. That lesson may be the most valuable outcome of all.

Negotiation, at its best, is not about defeating the other side. It is about navigating differences in a way that allows progress to continue. The world does not run on perfect alignment. It runs on the ability of people with competing priorities to find workable paths forward. This is true on job sites, in boardrooms, in communities, and in families. And, it is why negotiation will always remain an essential professional skill.

The chapters in this book have explored Principles, Pitfalls, and practical Pointers drawn from real negotiations and mediations. The goal has not been to present a rigid formula. Negotiation rarely follows scripts. Instead, the aim has been to highlight patterns and the recurring dynamics that shape how people respond to pressure, uncertainty, and perceived loss.

Recognizing those patterns is what separates experienced negotiators from inexperienced ones. But knowledge alone is not enough. The real value of these principles emerges only when they are practiced consistently over time. Negotiation is a craft refined through observation, reflection, and deliberate improvement. Each difficult conversation offers an opportunity to learn something about human behavior and about one's own leadership.

Those who approach negotiation with humility continue to grow throughout their careers. Those who believe they have already mastered it often stop learning precisely when the stakes become highest.

So, the final message of this book is simple. Play the long game.

Protect your credibility as if it were a strategic asset, because it is. Recognize the responsibility that accompanies influence. And teach the next generation of leaders that negotiation is not a contest of clever tactics but a discipline of judgment, patience, and perspective.

If future leaders understand that, they will not merely negotiate more effectively. They will lead more wisely.

C. Richard Barnes

ABOUT THE AUTHOR

Richard Barnes is President of C. Richard Barnes and Associates, LLC, a consulting firm which provides dispute resolution services, dispute resolution systems design, workforce training and development, facilitation, leadership coaching and negotiation skills training to a cross-section of industry, labor, private, public and service organizations, both nationally and internationally.

Immediately prior to forming his company, he was the Executive Director of the W. J. Usery Center for the Workplace at Georgia State University in Atlanta, Georgia. For seventeen years preceding his tenure at Georgia State, Richard served as a Federal Mediator with the Federal Mediation and Conciliation Service (FMCS), with seven of those years in executive management.

In 1998, President Clinton appointed Richard to serve as the 14th Director of FMCS. Once confirmed by the U.S. Senate, he became the first career mediator in FMCS history to receive both the Presidential Appointment and Senate Confirmation, a testament to his vast experience in leadership development, strategic negotiations and dispute resolution processes. His second Presidential Appointment to the National Partnership Council again recognized his commitment and expertise in developing and implementing positive workplace change initiatives.

As Director of FMCS, Richard was responsible for the management of our nation's Federal Mediators in all fifty states, Puerto Rico, the U.S. Virgin Islands, Guam and the Panama Canal. As both Director and Deputy Director, he led mediation teams that resolved some of our nation's most significant, intense and protracted labor-management disputes.

In his early years with FMCS, Richard served as the Alternative Dispute Resolution Coordinator and as Preventive Mediation Coordinator for the Southern Region of the U.S. During his tenure as the Alternative Dispute Resolution Coordinator, he conducted complex multi-party regulatory negotiations, and disputes involving the Panama Canal. Richard was subsequently selected as the FMCS District Director for the Atlanta District and soon promoted to Southern Regional Director. Shortly thereafter, he was selected as the Deputy Director for Field Operations in Washington, D.C. and in this position played a pivotal role in the strategic redirection of FMCS, a five-year reinvention process that realigned the agency, its services and personnel, to meet the changing needs of the labor relations and conflict resolution communities throughout the United States.

Richard is an internationally recognized mediator, facilitator, skills trainer and speaker and advances the practice of dispute resolution through his public/private partnership and role as an Adjunct professor at Kennesaw State University's Masters of Science in Conflict Resolution program. Richard serves as the facilitator for the Partnering Program of the National Electrical Contractors Association (NECA) and the International Brotherhood of Electrical Workers (IBEW). Recently, he developed a year-long experiential leadership program that was adopted by the Electrical Training ALLIANCE as their national leadership development program. Richard currently serves as the Faculty Chair for this program known as the VOLT Leadership Academy.

A native of Chattanooga, Tennessee, Richard is a veteran of the U.S. Army and served three years as an instructor at the Medical Field Service School at Brooke Army Medical Center, Fort Sam Houston, Texas. He is a graduate of the U.S. Army's prestigious Faculty Development Program and a graduate of Antioch University and the George Meany Center for Labor Studies. Richard holds undergraduate and advanced degrees in Labor Studies and Organizational Leadership. Richard and his wife Audrey reside in the Atlanta, Georgia area.

www.ingramcontent.com/pod-product-compliance
Lightning Source LLC
LaVergne TN
LVHW090549110826
845146LV00001B/74
* 9 7 9 8 9 9 5 3 8 6 7 1 1 *